SOUTH DEVON COLLEGE
LIBRARY

* 6 6 6 5 1 *

KT-149-230

Racial Discrimination

ISSUES FOR THE NINETIES

Volume 6

Editor

Craig Donnellan

 **Independence**

Educational Publishers
Cambridge

SOUTH DEVON COLLEGE
LIBRARY

SOUTH DEVON COLL. LIB.

ACC 66651 · CLASS 305.8 SIS

First published by Independence
PO Box 295
Cambridge CB1 3XP

© Craig Donnellan 1995

Copyright
This book is sold subject to the condition that it shall not,
by way of trade or otherwise, be lent, resold, hired out or otherwise
circulated in any form of binding or cover other than that in which it is published
without the publisher's prior consent.

Photocopy licence
The material in this book is protected by copyright. However, the purchaser
is free to make multiple copies of particular articles for instructional purposes
for immediate use within the purchasing institution. Making
copies of the entire book is not permitted.

British Library Cataloguing in Publication Data
Racial Discrimination – (Issues for the Nineties Series)
I. Donnellan, Craig II. Series
305.8

ISBN 1 872995 61 6

Printed in Great Britain
at City Print (Milton Keynes) Ltd
Bletchley, Milton Keynes

Cover
The cartoon on the front cover is by
the artist, Ken Pyne

Typeset by
Martyn Lusher Artwork, Cambridge

CONTENTS

Introduction

Racial Discrimination is the sixth volume in the series: **Issues For The Nineties**. The aim of this series is to offer up-to-date information about important issues in our world.

Racial Discrimination examines the issues of racial discrimination and racial violence. The information comes from a wide variety of sources and includes:

Government reports and statistics
Newspaper reports and features
Magazine articles and surveys
Literature from lobby groups
and charitable organisations.

It is hoped that, as you read about the many aspects of the issues explored in this book, you will critically evaluate the information presented. It is important that you decide whether you are being presented with facts or opinions. Does the writer give a biased or an unbiased report? If an opinion is being expressed, do you agree with the writer?

Racial Discrimination offers a useful starting point for those who need convenient access to information about the many issues involved. However, it is only a starting point. At the back of the book is a list of organisations which you may want to contact for further information.

*****

Racism and its roots

Racism is treating one group of people less favourably than another because of colour, religious belief, or ethnic origin. It was once widely held that human beings belonged to different 'races' of people, which were defined according to physical characteristics. Racism is rooted in the belief that some 'races' are superior to others. Feelings of racial superiority led Europeans to colonise countries in Asia, Africa, the Americas and the Caribbean, and exploit their economies.

Britain – home to people from many different cultures

At different times throughout history, people from many parts of the world have come to Britain and settled here. The first Jews arrived more than 1,000 years ago and Irish people came fleeing famine in the 1840s, and looking for work in the 1950s. Between the 15th and the 19th centuries, thousands of Africans were brought to Britain as slaves, seamen or servants of the wealthy. People from India, Pakistan, Bangladesh and the Caribbean were invited after World War II to do the jobs for which there were too few British workers.

A multicultural society

Britain, for most of its history, has been a multicultural society, with a host of people from minority ethnic groups making important contributions to every area of national life. A few facts about the make-up of Britain's population:

- According to the 1991 census, 5.5% of the population in Britain are from ethnic minorities, of which the largest group is Irish.

- Almost 50% of Britain's ethnic minority population were born here; about 75% are British citizens.
- Apart from English, 13 other languages are spoken by at least 100,000 people: Arabic, Bengali, Chinese, Greek, Gujarati, Hindi, Italian, Polish, Punjabi, Spanish, Turkish, Urdu, and Welsh.

The experience of racism

Racism can be experienced personally, through jokes, graffiti, abuse and violence, and discrimination from other people. It can also be experienced institutionally – that is, by the discrimination of a society's laws and social policies, such as being denied access to education, jobs, housing, and other services.

When people from Africa, the Caribbean and Asia arrived in Britain during the 1940s, they were confronted with open hostility. In the late 1950s and 60s, Black and Asian people were often subjected to name-calling and physical attacks, and many landlords and landladies put up signs saying 'No Blacks, No Irish, No dogs'. And all because they were 'different'. Things like this still happen today.

Racism in Britain today

- In a 1991 survey of 400 ethnic minority household in Preston, 74% said that at least one member had experienced racial harassment in the previous two years.
- Black people in Britain are twice as likely to be jobless as white people, and when they have a job, it is more likely to be low-paid, semi-skilled or unskilled work.

Racism and the law

The 1976 Race Relations Act makes racial discrimination unlawful. The law, however, cannot do a lot about prejudice – how people think or feel about others. The Commission for Racial Equality was set up to enforce the Race Relations Act. The 86 Racial Equality Councils around the country give support and advice to people who are discriminated against.

Gift or threat?

Growing up in multicultural societies gives everyone the chance to experience the rich diversity of human life and different ways of looking at the world. Here are just a few of the things that people from other places have brought to Britain:

- Religion – Buddhism, Judaism, Islam, Hinduism, Sikhism and, long ago, even Christianity itself.
- Music and dance – Caribbean calypso and reggae, bhangra and many other styles from Asia, a huge range of African music, and soul, blues and jazz from the black American tradition.
- Food – from curries to kebabs, stir-fries to pizzas, and a host of exotic fruit and vegetables.
- Clothes – the different textures, colours and styles of clothes from other cultures, and their influence on high-street fashions.

© CAFOD (Catholic Fund for Overseas Development)
January, 1995

Race – the facts

The scars of race are deep and divisive. They can be seen in all parts of the world, in all walks of life

Violence

Racist attacks are on the increase in many parts of the world.

Indigenous Canadians are six times more likely to be murdered than other Canadians.[1]

In the UK, Asians are 50 times and West Indians 36 times more likely than whites to be victims of racial violence.[14]

In the US, 6 out of every 10 hate crimes had a racial motive and a further 1 in 10 an ethnic motive. 36% were anti-black, 21% anti-white and 13% anti-Jewish.[15]

Imprisonment and exile

Belonging to the 'wrong' group increases the chances of imprisonment and asylum rejection.

Most of the world's 15 million refugees come from the South and seek refuge in neighbouring countries. One person in 10 was a refugee in Malawi in July 1993, compared to one in 5,000 in the UK. The rate of asylum refusal on appeal in the UK has risen from 14% to 72%.[19]

Work

Racial prejudice affects access to jobs.

Canada – indigenous people are twice as likely to be jobless as the rest of the population.

US – blacks are twice as likely to be jobless as whites.[1]

UK – ethnic minorities are twice as likely to be jobless. Ethnic minority women are three times as likely to be jobless as other women.[2]

Australia – Aboriginal people are more than three times as likely to be jobless as the general population.[3]

But in India 10% of higher level jobs in the public sector now go to people from the Scheduled Castes (more than 16% of the total population) compared with only 3.5% in 1972.[4]

Health, wealth & housing

How we live, where we live and how long we live may often be determined by race.

In the US

Nearly 50% of the black population live in polluted areas, compared to 30% of the white population.[1]

40% of Native Americans live below the poverty line. 37% die before the age of 45.[10] They are 10 times as likely to die of alcohol abuse.[11]

In Australia

Aboriginal people's life expectancy is 15 years lower than the rest of the population. Infant mortality is three times higher.[3]

The suicide rate is six times higher.[10]

Aboriginal family income is about half the Australian average.[12]

In South Africa

The white 14% of the population owns almost 90% of the land.

Life expectancy for whites is 73 years, for blacks 57. Infant mortality among whites is 18 per 1,000; among blacks, 57 per 1,000.[9]

In the UK

People from ethnic minorities are four times more likely to be homeless in London than whites.[13]

Strife & genocide

Half of the world's states have recently experienced inter-ethnic strife.

The result has been:
- In Afghanistan one in six people has been disabled by a landmine.
- In Zaire more than 800,000 people have been displaced.
- In Sri Lanka more than 14,000 have died in clashes between Tamils and Sinhalese.
- In former Yugoslavia more than 130,000 people have been killed since 1991.[1]
- Up to 50,000 people were killed in Burundi in 1993.[20]
- In Rwanda the attempted genocide of Tutsis has resulted in an estimated 200,000 – 500,000 deaths.
- In Brazil an average of one tribe a year has been wiped out since 1900.[10]

Education

Discrimination affects the languages we speak and the education we get.

Fewer than 5% of the world's languages are given official recognition by governments.[5] No more than 100 people can speak Japan's indigenous Ainu language fluently.[6]

Sources:
[1] UNDP *Human Development Report*, 1994.
[2] 1991 Census: Crown copyright. Through NEMDA.
[3] NSW Task Force on Aboriginal Health, 1987.
[4] *India Today*, 30 April, 1994.
[5] Minority Rights Group.
[6] *COLORS* 4, 1993.
[7] Indian Census 1991.
[8] Philip Searne, *The Maya of Guatemala*, MRG, London, forthcoming.
[9] *Choices*, UNDP, June 1994.
[10] Survival International.
[11] *Talking Stick* 1, 1993.
[12] 1986 Census, Australian Bureau of Statistics.
[13] *Race through the 90s*, Council for Racial Equality and BBC, 1993.
[14] Institute of Race Relations.
[15] *Uniform Crime Report*, March 1994, FBI, reported by Center for Democratic Renewal.
[16] Home Office Statistical Bulletin 9/91. Through NEMDA.
[17] Julian Berger. *The Gala Atlas of First Peoples*, 1990.
[18] Bureau of Justice Statistics, in *New Statesman & Society*, 1 April 1994.
[19] WUS Update, June 1994.
[20] UNHCR *Information Bulletin*, 10 December 1993.

© *New Internationalist*
October, 1994

Without prejudice

Listen to what some people say and you would think this country was 'overrun' with five, ten, 20 million black and Asian people, that they are living in good homes and holding decent jobs while 'we' are on the dole queue.

These things are as easy to repeat as they are untrue. Next time you hear the things they say, remember the facts we give you here.

They say...

They're still flooding in when the country's crowded with millions of them.

Fact

Immigration is strictly controlled and relatively few people are allowed in to settle. More people leave Britain to live abroad than come to live here.

Of those who have come to live in Britain 61% are white.

Only 1 in 20 people living in Britain are black or Asian, that's 5%.

Some – including politicians – would have you believe there is massive immigration into this country. It's nonsense. Britain has some of the strictest immigration controls in the world and it's been like that for a quarter of a century.

Others would have you think that there are many millions of black and Asian people living in this country. Untrue. The figures speak for themselves. The total number of black and Asian people living in Britain is now 3 million or 5.5% of the total.

In the 32 years since records started, only in five years have more people settled in Britain than have gone abroad. They are 1962, 1972, 1983, 1984, 1985.

They say...

They should learn to be British like us.

Fact

Nearly half the black and Asian people living here were born in Britain.

This country is their home as much as it is that of anyone else born here. Everyone living here has a right to be treated decently and fairly. And anyway, who is 'British?' Is it the Scots, or the Welsh or the English? Or is it those from Yorkshire or those who speak like a Cockney?

We are all proud of ourselves, of who we are and where we come from.

The differences are what makes life in Britain so rich and exciting. We don't all have to be the same to be able to share pride in the people of this country – and pride in working together to make it a better place.

People abroad are quite clear who they see as 'British.' They don't say you can't be British unless you support the England cricket team. For them the British person they know is now as likely to be Linford Christie winning a gold medal in the Olympics as it is to be John Major.

Of course, it is not always easy to get on with new differences. But Chinese take-aways, black music and the Asian shops are in our streets and communities because they are needed.

They say...

They're taking our jobs . . .

Fact

Black, Asian or Irish people are more likely to be unemployed than the average. They are also more likely to be in a lower paid job and one using lower skills.

Far from 'taking our jobs,' such workers are often doing jobs others have chosen not to do, perhaps because they are too dirty, too hard or the wages are too low.

Asian or black people are not stuck in these jobs because they do not have the skills or the education to do better. People in groups such as Bangladeshis are four times more likely than whites to end up in the dole queue. And figures show that the gap between unemployment rates for whites on the one hand and black and Asian groups on the other, gets larger as one goes up the skills ladder.

So, for instance, 22% of Pakistanis with A-levels or above are unemployed. For whites the figure is only 5%.

WHEN IT COMES TO RACISM I SEE EVERYTHING IN BLACK AND WHITE

Ken Pyne

They say...

The race relations laws give special favours to black and Asian people . . .

Fact

Each year white people win cases in courts and tribunals using the Race Relations Act. It gives privileges to no one, only rights to all.

In this country there are no quotas for jobs, no reserved places. People who have jobs where things have been run properly under the Race Relations Act have them because they deserve them. The Act makes discrimination against the law – you can't be denied a job because you are Asian or because you are white.

Only in exceptional cases does it let someone get a job because they are white, black, Chinese or whatever. These are simple things like being a waiter in a Chinese restaurant, acting the part of Winston Churchill or taking care of elderly Bangladeshi women who speak very little English.

It's where the Act is ignored that things become unfair. Companies which follow real equal opportunities are the most efficient, get the best staff for the job, treat all their staff better and are the ones on the look out for the ways to get better still.

They say...

They're sponging off the welfare state . . .

Fact

Asian and black people use the benefit system less than whites – and they are less likely to claim the benefits they have a right to.

People from ethnic minorities come off worse throughout the benefits system.

They are less likely to be claiming benefits like pensions because they are generally younger than whites but when they do go to the benefits system they run into all sorts of problems.

Research has shown that they are less likely to be claiming the benefits they have a right to – for some this will be because of the difficulty of filling in complex forms in English when it is not their first language, for others it may be because of racism in the benefits system.

Black and Asian people are more likely to be refused benefits than whites and face longer delays than white claimants before they get a decision in their favour.

They say...

They jump the housing queues . . .

Fact

Local councils and housing associations give homes on the basis of careful rules, which means homes go to those who need them, white or black.

If there is a problem it is the other way round – black and Asian people get a rougher deal. They're more likely to end up homeless. The homes they do get are more likely to be run down or overcrowded. Sometimes the rules that local councils lay down have made it harder for them to get decent housing than is the case for whites.

Just take one figure – that for households with one or more bedroom below standard. For whites only 2% of households are covered. For Pakistanis and Bangladeshis the figure soars to 28%.

If you are black or Asian you are more likely than a white person to be living in a home built before 1945, one that is terraced rather than semi-detached or detached, and one that is overcrowded. That last problem affects 35% of Asians but only 3% of whites.

They say...

They have too many children . . .

Fact

Family sizes are falling for all groups except Bangladeshis – for some Afro-Caribbeans the number of children for each adult is now lower than for whites.

Families come in all sorts of shapes and sizes – some of us, white or black, live with in-laws, grand-parents, and cousins while others live on their own. Some cannot understand how people can cope with more than two adults in the same house, others don't understand what they see as the cruelty of pushing the elderly into the lonely life of a single flat.

Only in the case of Bangladeshis have families grown in size over the past ten years. For all other ethnic minorities family sizes are falling faster than for whites.

They say...

They are not as bright as we are . . .

Fact

School exam results now show that whites are no longer always in the lead – other groups are there with them. Some studies show Afro-Caribbean girls do best of all.

The one about the thick Paddy still gets a laugh, but the days are long gone when anybody seriously suggested that it was actually true. Many people from different minority groups still have problems in the education system – discrimination and different treatment has not been overcome.

But at the end of the day the exam results tell their own tale.

They say...

They're all muggers or crack dealers . . .

Fact

Black and Asian people are more likely to be victims of crime and less likely to be criminals than whites.

Crime is one of the big problems in this country today. It affects us all. The figures show that people who are black or Asian are more likely to be the victims of crimes than are whites.

And they are the targets of a particular problem – racial violence. The latest Home Office figures show that black and Asian people in Britain suffer some 110,000 racially motivated assaults, threats or acts of vandalism each year with many, many more acts of abuse and harassment that go unrecorded.

People are still being attacked and seriously injured, in some cases even murdered, solely because of the colour of their skin.

Yet police figures show that some, particularly young black men, are more likely than whites to be stopped and questioned but never charged with any offence.

Don't just listen . . .

Don't just sit and listen to the things people say. Take it up with them and try to get them to think and not just repeat prejudices they have picked up from others.

1 Insults
If you hear someone using racist insults or even threatening and harassing others just because of their colour, don't ignore it. Let both sides know that you disagree with racism. Let the person who is doing it know they are doing something you think is wrong. Let the victims know they are not on their own and that you will help them if necessary.

2 Discrimination
If you think your employer is discriminating against someone because of their race, raise the matter with a trade union, the personnel manager – or with the person you think is the target of the discrimination. Make a careful note of what happened, it could help someone gain their rights.

3 Harassment
Racial attacks are crimes. If you see acts of violence or intimidation directed against people because of their race go to the police and act as a witness.

4 Be sensible
Don't try to solve all the problems of the world on your own. If you respond to someone who is using racial insults against a colleague at work or someone in the street, do so with care and dignity. Remember that you are trying to help the person the abuse is directed against.

5 Get advice
There are many specialist advice centres which can help – there is usually a citizens' advice bureau within reach, many towns have a racial equality council and you can always ring the Commission for Racial Equality.

6 Spread the word
If you want more information on this subject contact the CRE at Elliot House, 10 Allington Street, London SW1E 5EH or ring through to 071 828 7022 and ask for Publications. Use the same number and ask for information to get further details on who to contact.

● This article was produced by the Commission for Racial Equality in partnership with BBC Radio 1.
© The Commission for Racial Equality (CRE) and BBC June, 1994

We may be Black but please don't call us British

Black people hate being called British, according to a new report. Despite being born and bred in Britain, with many even feeling that they are British, the phrase sticks in their throats.

Young Black people with British passports are more likely to call themselves 'Black'. The older generation who came to Britain in the 50s prefer to be called West Indian – but never British.

It is a backlash after years of racial violence, discrimination and feeling like second class citizens, the independent Policy Studies Institute report *Changing Ethnic Identities* found.

Author Tariq Modood said: 'It is clear the ethnic identities are a product of racial exclusion as well as ethnic pride and loyalty to one's family. They should, however, be a product of positive not negative forces.'

The main problem is that Britain's two generations of Black people find that being proud of their heritage and passing it on to their children is incompatible with being British.

'The majority of White people believed that only White people could be British,' the report concludes. 'This racism, rather than any sense of distinctive ethnic heritage was seen as an obstacle to feelings of unity with the White British majority.'

Mr Modood said: 'We need to reject the racism that says only White people can be British. We should encourage emergent 'hyphenated' identities such as Black-British and British-Pakistani and accept that there are a variety of ways of being British.'
© The Voice January, 1995

'They all look the same to me...'

Combating racism through language

Do they mean me?

Language is a social institution, and as such it is constrained and influenced by what is happening in society.

In its turn, language constrains and influences development and progression in society. Our attitudes are reflected in our choices of language.

We can choose to dehumanise and focus attention on that one aspect of an individual by using terms such as 'blacks'. But when we choose to remind the speaker that people are people first by saying 'black people' we are seeing people in their entirety.

Have you noticed that words containing 'black' have negative connotations? . . . black mood, blacklisted, black sheep of the family, black magic . . . What examples can you think of?

On the other hand, white is seen as pure, good, and clean, e.g. white christmas (joy), white wedding (virginity).

Discrimination is reinforced by our language. Black people are saying that care should be taken to choose terms that value rather than devalue them as individuals.

For example, the word coloured was and is still used to describe certain racial groups by a white ruling elite, and generally represented a condescending frame of mind towards those it referred to. It also represented a 'colour-blind' approach by white people and a resistance to seeing black people for who they truly are.

The adjective 'black' is chosen by black people themselves as a statement of pride. It represents a statement of endorsement and legitimation by those who use it.

Anti-racist youth work – some useful definitions

Ways of describing people:

BLACK is the general term used throughout this article to refer to

So next time, how about

	Instead of
Black person	coloured
mixed race	half-caste
Black people	blacks
Chinese	chink

What examples can you think of?

Language perpetuates stereotypes, stereotypes perpetuate racism.

Mind your language!

those who, because of their race, colour or ethnic origin, are visibly identifiable as different from the ethnic majority. The term encompasses people from a wide range of communities with huge cultural, social, linguistic, religious, and in some cases, political differences, and includes third or fourth generation African-Caribbeans and Asians, as well as refugees from Vietnam, Somalia or Uganda.

Some would argue that the term denies these differences and fails to acknowledge the importance of people's national identity. It is nevertheless a convenient way of emphasising black people's shared experience as identifiable targets and victims of racism, with its common roots in the history of slavery and/or colonialism. It also helps to remind us of the common anti-racist strategies and political responses which

The word coloured was and is still used to describe certain racial groups by a white ruling elitetowards those it referred to.

are needed to combat it. Most important of all, it is a term with which most black people identify, once they recognise that it refers to a shared political experience rather than to skin tone.

COLOURED is generally considered to be a derogatory term because it ignores the fact that everyone has coloured skin pigmentation, and assumes that whiteness is the norm with which everyone who is not white should be compared. It is particularly offensive because of its associations with the Apartheid system in South Africa, which classified the non-white population as blacks, Indians or 'coloureds' – and above all, it is not the word black people would choose to describe themselves.

PEOPLE OF COLOUR is the umbrella term used in the United States to refer to descendants of (non-white) immigrant and slave communities such as African Americans, Puerto Ricans and Vietnamese. For the reasons given above (see 'coloured') it hasn't caught on here.

HALF-CASTE is also considered a negative term. It implies that the person being described is in some way inadequate or incomplete and, like Mulatto (originally a Spanish term for a cross between an ass and a mule), it ignores national identity.

MIXED RACE is nowadays the term preferred by most people of mixed parentage, because it highlights the race factor – and hence the racism – which invariably affects their lives. Many people of mixed race also choose to identify themselves as black (because one white parent makes no difference to a racist), or by their parents' nationality (e.g. Anglo-Nigerian, Afro-British etc.).

© SCADU
February, 1994

What is the Commission for Racial Equality?

The Commission for Racial Equality (CRE) was set up by the 1976 Race Relations Act. It is funded by an annual grant from the Home Office, but works independently of Government. It is run by Commissioners appointed by the Home Secretary, and has support from all the main political parties.

The duties of the CRE are to work towards the elimination of racial discrimination, to promote equal opportunities and good race relations, and to monitor the way the Act is working.

The Commission for Racial Equality is working for a just society which gives everyone an equal chance to learn, work and live free from discrimination and prejudice, and from the fear of racial harassment and violence.

The Race Relations Act 1976 covers discrimination on the grounds of a person's colour, race, nationality, citizenship, and ethnic or national origin. The CRE is therefore concerned with all victims of racial discrimination, irrespective of their colour, race, or nationality.

Why the CRE exists

Racial discrimination can occur in many different ways. It may be a direct refusal to give someone a job, or accommodation, or a place on a college course, just because of the colour of their skin or their nationality. It may be more subtle. Telling job applicants that they must have a degree from a 'British University' may discriminate indirectly against any applicants educated overseas.

Much of the discrimination that occurs is based on 'colour', and is directed against

COMMISSION FOR RACIAL EQUALITY

the 'visible' minorities – people of Asian, African, Caribbean and Chinese origin. The CRE is concerned, however, about anyone who may have experienced racial discrimination, whatever their background. White people, Irish people, Gypsies, and other ethnic or national groups are covered equally by the Race Relations Act.

It is sometimes said that claims of racial discrimination and injustice are exaggerated, and that organisations like the CRE only make things worse by dwelling on problems that barely exist. The fact is that racial discrimination, injustice, harassment and even violent attacks are daily experiences for many people from ethnic minority groups living in Britain today:

- The Home Office has accepted estimates that there may be as many as 130,000 racial incidents in a year.
- People from ethnic minorities are twice as likely as white people to be unemployed.
- Ethnic minority families are three times more likely to be homeless.

Society cannot afford to ignore these problems. The CRE is the *only* Government appointed body in the country with a statutory power to enforce the Race Relations Act. It is the CRE's duty to draw attention to racial discrimination wherever it occurs.

What the CRE does

The CRE's activities cover employment, training, housing, health, social services, education, trade unions, the criminal justice system, and the way in which goods and services are provided to the public. We also help other agencies take action on racial harassment and attacks.

Using the law

Anyone who thinks they have suffered racial discrimination has the right to take legal action in a court or industrial tribunal. The CRE can help complainants directly, or it can put them in touch with other agencies.

The CRE also has the power to conduct formal investigations of companies and organisations where there is evidence of discrimination. If the CRE finds discrimination, it can take steps to see that it is stopped. The CRE can also take action on discriminatory advertisements, and in cases where people have been instructed, or put under pressure, to discriminate.

Photo: David Hoffman

Promoting equal opportunities and good race relations

The CRE advises a variety of agencies on how to avoid discrimination, and give everyone an equal chance – Training and Enterprise Councils, local authorities, employers, health and education authorities, the police, housing departments, etc. The CRE also publishes guides and codes of practice to help organisations achieve equal opportunities.

The CRE is concerned with all victims of racial discrimination

The CRE advises, and makes representations to, Government on race issues. It also keeps MPs, political parties, national organisations and institutions, and the media informed.

Working with others

The CRE cannot achieve a just society on its own. We work closely with organisations and institutions at a national, regional and local level, including a network of racial equality councils (RECs), which we also help to fund. The RECs are managed by representatives of community groups, voluntary and statutory organisations, and individuals who support their aims.

© Commission for Racial Equality

Restaurants to pay £30m to victims of racism

Denny's restaurant chain has agreed to pay $46 million (£30 million) to thousands of black patrons who were discriminated against around America.

The chain, with 1,500 restaurants, said it would settle 4,300 complaints, pay more than $8.7 million (£5.8 million) in lawyers' fees for the plaintiffs, retrain employees and conduct random checks of its premises.

The Justice Department determined that some black clients at Denny's were refused service while others were asked to pay a cover charge, pay in advance or meet other conditions not required of white patrons.

The lawsuits stemmed from complaints filed by six black Secret Service agents assigned to President Clinton, who on April 1 last year were not served for 55 minutes at a Denny's in Annapolis, Maryland, while 15 white colleagues received second and third helpings in the same time. Meanwhile, a client in California complained that in 1991 his daughter was refused a free dinner on her 13th birthday as the chain had advertised, despite supplying proof of her age.

The Annapolis case spawned 1,300 bias complaints in 49 states. Denny's has agreed to pay the six agents £23,300 each and divide £11.5 million among other victims.

The California incident led to 3,000 complaints, which Denny's has settled. It has agreed to pay £16,600 to 40 plaintiffs, with another £18 million to be divided among other victims. Another £300,000 will be paid to the 132-member Martin Luther King Jr Choir who were denied service at two Virginia restaurants.

'We have no policy and no practice to discriminate against anyone. If there were situations where there was [discrimination], we apologise for that,' Mr Jerome Richardson, chairman of Flagstar Companies Incorporated, Denny's parent company, said at a press conference. – AFP

© The Telegraph Plc
May, 1994

Blacks stranded at back of jobs queue

Youngsters face bleak work outlook as Bernie Grant blames dead-end training schemes and warns of trouble ahead

By Anthony Bevins and Dean Nelson

Hard evidence that young blacks are at the bottom of the employment pile is provided by the latest Government survey of Youth Training leavers. The figures show that young blacks fare worse than the disabled when it comes to finding jobs.

The survey of those who took Youth Training courses between December 1992 and January last year shows that only one in four young blacks found jobs, compared with a third of disabled trainees and half of whites.

Bernie Grant, Labour MP for Tottenham, said the figures were 'horrific' and warned of a wave of riots if the Government did not take urgent measures to tackle black unemployment.

The figures are published against a background of increasing Government concern at levels of black unemployment and calls from Labour for urgent action to help young urban blacks into work. In London, 62 per cent of black men between 16 and 24 are unemployed, compared with 20 per cent of whites in the same age group.

The Department of Employment analysis of Youth Training leavers, in response to Commons questions from shadow spokeswoman Harriet Harman, also shows that women are more likely to find work than men.

But while 45 per cent of men and women trainees obtained full-time jobs, 7 per cent of the women went into part-time employment, compared with 3 per cent of men. While 25 per cent of the women remained unemployed, 28 per cent of the men were left without work.

Black community leaders said the figures confirmed anecdotal evidence that Youth Training was failing black job seekers. They said black youths faced racial discrimination on Youth Training courses through poor career guidance.

Mr Grant said: 'London is a giant blackspot for unemployment, and the TECs (training and enterprise councils) must take their share of the blame. In black, working-class areas they offer courses in bartending. In middle-class areas, it's computer studies.'

Elaine Smith of Finsbury Park Community Trust in north London said young blacks were often advised to take construction skill courses with no opportunity of gaining work experience. 'I worked in Youth Training for six years and what happened was that the young black

Figures from the CRE show that:

Ethnic minorities comprise 5.9 % of the working population. But ...

in the Civil Service they make up just 5.2% of the workforce,

in the fire service they make up just one per cent of the workforce,

in the Army they make up less than one per cent of new recruits, and

in the Metropolitan Police, at the end of 1993, there were a total of 651 officers from ethnic minorities in a total strength of 29,000. This represents 2.3% of the total, whereas the ethnic minorities in London make up 18% of the population.

men were trapped in a workshop for six months while the white trainees would do four days a week with local employers and only one day at college. The blacks were told they needed all the workshop training they could get. This disparity in finding jobs reflects the guidance young blacks are being given.'

The Trust has pioneered one of Britain's most successful schemes for easing black people into full-time jobs, by striking an agreement with W H Smith to provide local job-seekers to work unpaid for three months, with guaranteed jobs if they prove their ability. They receive training, advice and childcare support from the Trust, which is supported by local authority and European Social Fund grants.

The approach is to challenge employers' preconceptions that black people are lazy and unreliable. Its success rate contrasts starkly with the Government's Youth Training figures: more than 70 per cent of clients find full-time jobs and more than 60 per cent of clients are black.

'The training we provide gives people a track record. We sell the skills of black people to employers to overcome their prejudice. It's more of a problem with black men. Employers think they will have no commitment. But when they realise these people are giving it everything, working every day for just their benefits, it changes their attitude,' said Ms Smith.

'Youth Training doesn't cater for black people's needs. It is focused on qualifications, rather than getting jobs. Young blacks need someone to say, "here's an untapped source of talent".'

© *Observer*
February, 1995

Equality for all

Winning race equality at work

Getting started

This article is a practical guide to negotiating race equality at work. It includes handy references to the law, as well as examples of agreements won by Transport and General Workers Union (T&G) representatives in a range of workplaces up and down the country.

On page 39 of this book you will find a list of useful contacts who can provide extra help, whether that's advice on how to draft a new agreement or what to expect if you represent a member at an Industrial Tribunal.

Winning race equality in the workplace is one of the most important challenges facing trade unions today. This article will help you get started.

As a matter of fact

The T&G estimates that about one in ten members are black or belong to an ethnic minority. Black women are more likely to belong to a union than white women while the reverse is true for men. (Source: *Labour Force Survey*, 1989)

Recruitment, promotion and selection

The 'colour bar' is still alive and kicking in British industry. Word of mouth and other informal methods of recruitment and promotion mean that black people may never get the chance to compete for a job. But a failure to advertise openly could be against the law. The Commission for Racial Equality (CRE) Code of Practice says; 'employers should not confine advertisements to those areas or publications which would exclude or disproportionately reduce the numbers of applicants from a particular racial group.' (CRE Code 1.6 a)

- Where an employer has an internal advertising procedure, try winning agreement to simultaneous internal and external advertising.

- Urge the employer to advertise jobs in the black press as a way of increasing applications from black people. But remind them not to expect instant results. It takes a while for a workplace with a 'whites-only' reputation to build up credibility as an equal opportunity employer.

- Ads should carry an equal opportunity commitment and can encourage under-represented groups to apply. They should also make it crystal clear that comparable qualifications and skills gained abroad are acceptable.

- Tell the employer to avoid making unnecessary requirements, such as length of residence or experience, which may deter black people from applying.

- If your employer recruits through a particular employment agency, job centre or school, check whether it means that black people are less likely to apply.

- Clear job descriptions and person specifications are vital. Staff involved in short-listing and interviewing should be informed of selection criteria and given appropriate training on the effects of prejudice on selection decisions.

As a matter of fact...

About one third of private employers discriminate against black applicants by refusing them an interview while offering one to equally qualified whites. (Source: Employment Institute, *Economic Report*, June 1990)

Black people are one and a half times more likely to be unemployed than whites.

Passing the test

IQ, 'psychometric' and personality tests are employers' latest recruitment fad. The quasi-scientific appearance of such tests may conceal inbuilt race bias. In a recent case backed by the CRE, a British Rail test based on principles common throughout industry was shown to discriminate against people who speak English as a second language.

- Check that selection tests and criteria are strictly related to job requirements and are not designed in such a way as to make it harder for ethnic minority groups to pass. (CRE Code 1.13)

As a matter of fact . . .

Black people are one and a half times more likely to be unemployed than whites. The unemployment rate for black youth is double that for whites. (Source: *Employment Gazette*, February, April 1991)

Genuine occupational qualification

Selection on racial grounds is allowed in certain jobs where being of a particular racial group is a genuine occupational qualification for that job. The CRE Code of Practice gives the example of where a job involves providing a racial group with personal services promoting their welfare. (CRE Code 1.15)

The colour of money

The simple fact is that black workers are lower paid than whites. According to the PSI survey, 'Black and White in Britain', on average black men earn 85% of white men's gross weekly pay. Although the gap between black and white women's weekly earnings is much smaller, this is partly because black women work longer hours.

Black people are concentrated in the lowest paying industries and jobs. Unequal training and promotion opportunities confirm black workers' poor status. So, many of the tried and tested Union demands around ending low pay will directly benefit black workers.

But there is another problem negotiators need to address and that is the low value attached to black people's work. As with sex, a worker's race can colour society's view of how much a job is worth. Black women's work is often treated as the lowest skilled of all.

Ethnic monitoring of the pay and grading structure is vital. Over-representation of black workers in the lowest grades suggests that discrimination has occurred and is a powerful argument for positive action.

For example, at Ford's, black workers are concentrated in the lowest paying grades.

There is leverage in both the equal pay and race discrimination laws to tackle bias in pay (CRE Code 1.20) but the biggest gains can be won through negotiation using the checklist below:
- Find out where black workers are in the pay and grading structure.
- Aim to abolish or consolidate the lowest grades.

- Aim to improve basic pay.
- Look at how much black women earn and if you think there may be pay discrimination on the grounds of sex, use the equal value laws to back up your argument to management.

© *Transport & General Workers Union*
June, 1993

Ford of Britain hourly paid ethnic minority workers by grade

Grade	Total ethnic minority workers	Percentage of ethnic minority workers in grade
1	17	28.3
2	2469	23.5
3	2496	19.2
4	407	13.3
5	154	2.9
Technical trainees	58	6.4
Total in Ford of Britain	**5601**	**17.0**

From: *Ford of Britain, 1989 Equal Opportunities Report*

Report explodes A-level myth

Black students' results are up to scratch

The lack of Black students in higher education cannot be explained by poor A-levels, a new analysis of admissions data has revealed.

The research explodes long-held myths that Black and other ethnic minority students are not getting good enough grades and do not reach the standard required to get into university.

Tariq Modood, senior fellow at the independent Policy Studies Institute, north west London, who carried out the research, explained that in 1992, even when applicants in the clearing system had the same grades, the rates of acceptance still differed.

'We discovered that, regardless of how many students applied, some ethnic minority groups could be roughly divided into three groups.

'Black African, Indian and Bangladeshis had hardly any difference between their rate of entry and those of White students. Chinese and other Asians have a higher rate of entry than Whites whilst Pakistanis and Black Caribbeans have a significantly lower level of acceptance than Whites,' he said.

The results suggest that there may be indirect or direct discrimination in the system, but Mr Modood admits that he is unsure about the reason for the disparity. 'It is a mystery,' he said.

He continued: 'If three students with identical A-levels graded C, C, and D had applied to UCCA and PCAS (which oversee university and polytechnic admissions), the Chinese applicant would probably have gone to university; the White applicant would have been a border-line case; a Black Caribbean candidate would probably have gone to polytechnic (now new university).'

Dr Morgan Dalphinis, lecturer and curriculum manager at Handsworth Community College Network,

argues that the results pointed to the 'cultural cohesion' of each community rather than providing evidence of racial discrimination.

'As an ex-slave population our understanding has changed radically. There are lots more Black people doing A-levels... but Oxford and Cambridge are still viewed as un-known territory. Most Black people there are from overseas.

'The Chinese continue their pattern of setting a high value on themselves and their people. Even some of their literature considers the world as savages, including the Whites, and they have limited contact outside the Chinese community. They train to bring their skills back into their community.'

Despite these disparities, one in three young people now enters higher education.

© *Voice*
September, 1994

It's no joke when you can't get a job

Stopping somebody getting a job because they are black, Asian or Irish has been against the law for some 30 years. But it goes on every day. Black, Asian and Irish people are more likely to be unemployed than the average. They are also more likely to be in lower paid jobs

Waiting for a job

Earl Forbes had been working in hotels and restaurants for some years before he spotted the job in the Cosy View Bar and Diner. He knew the tricks of the trade and was a solid worker with no difficulty in getting good references.

The Cosy View was getting ready to start trading and they wanted front-of-house staff. Earl was called for an interview with the manager who asked him if he would cut his mini-dreadlocks. The manager said it was not a problem so far as he was concerned, but the company boss might not like it. The restaurant was to be a place with a 'fun theme' and they wanted staff who could 'fit in'.

Earl said, 'No way', went home and heard nothing. The Cosy View took on staff – all were white and most were less experienced than Earl. When the restaurant opened a couple of weeks later Earl noticed what had happened.

He went to the local racial equality council to ask their advice. They put him on to the CRE which gave him legal help for an industrial tribunal case. It was different to what Earl had expected. There were no wigs and robes, just three ordinary looking people on the tribunal and a relaxed, straightforward air to the discussion.

It was not the length of Earl's hair that had bothered the Cosy View. The boss himself had a pony tail. Indeed he said he thought the whole complaint was a joke. He was Jewish and Irish and 'knew all about discrimination'.

It was at that point that the chair of the tribunal got rather cross.

> *If he had been unemployed they could have made the restaurant compensate him at a full wage for every week he stayed on the dole queue*

'To those who bring them, complaints of race discrimination are no joke,' he said; 'It is no longer good enough for employers to declare they do not discriminate. They must take positive steps to make sure they are treating everyone fairly – and they must make sure that all their managers know how to do this.'

The tribunal awarded Earl £1,500 for 'injury to feelings' which the restaurant had to pay over. Because he did not lose any money by not getting the job, the tribunal could not award him compensation. If he had been unemployed they could have made the restaurant compensate him at a full wage for every week he stayed on the dole queue.

The above is an extract from *Without prejudice*.

© Commission for Racial Equality/BBC
June, 1994

Photo: David Hoffman

The unemployment rate for black youth is double that for whites

Ministers admit 60% of young black men jobless

By Barrie Clement
Labour Editor

More than six in ten young black men in London are out of work, according to data released by ministers yesterday.

Government critics saw the figures as the most stark statistical evidence yet of a breakdown in the social fabric of inner cities and called for urgent action to deal with the problem.

In a parliamentary answer to the labour Party frontbencher Harriet Harman, Philip Oppenheim, Employment Minister, revealed a Labour Force Survey estimate that 62 per cent of black men in London between 16 and 24 were unemployed.

The figures, based on the International Labour Organisation's definition of unemployment, also found that more than a third of black men of all ages in the capital were out of work. Just over a fifth of black women were jobless, according to estimates covering last summer.

Ms Harman, Labour's employment spokeswoman, said the statistics were 'truly shocking' and proved that a whole generation was outside the world of work. Many of the jobless had children themselves, she said. 'Children are growing up in families which have never known the security and dignity of work.'

Young black men were three times more likely to be jobless than young white men in London, one in five of whom was also out of work. 'It is clear that even steady improvement in the economy will not make a dent in unemployment among young black people – it has gone too deep,' she said.

Ms Harman called for specific action targeted on inner cities. Young black men needed the skills to get them into work and access to help in establishing small businesses, she said. 'A whole generation is in danger of being alienated from the rest of a society which appears to offer them little or no future. Society has an obligation to offer young people opportunities in life.'

Launching a report this week which showed that the country's largest employers paid only lip service to equal opportunities, Herman Ouseley, chairman of the Commission for Racial Equality, said all the top decision-makers in government and the private sector bore a responsibility for the plight of ethnic minorities.

© *The Independent* January, 1995

The Wood-Sheppard principles

Companies wishing to support race equality in employment are asked to give a general endorsement to these principles, to work progressively towards their implementation and to be willing to provide a modest response annually on their progress:

1 Adopt a detailed equal opportunities policy (EOP), preferably with assistance from the Commission for Racial Equality or a similar body.

2 Declare a clear intention to increase the representation of black and minority ethnic groups in their workforce, wherever there are underrepresented in relation to the local community.

3 Undertake positive action to improve the proportion of minorities in the workforce, to offset any imbalance caused by previous discrimination.

4 Practise effective ethnic monitoring of the EOP policy, with a regular review.

5 Use fair recruitment and selection processes, with clear objective criteria, avoiding reliance on 'word of mouth' or family contact methods.

6 Evolve comprehensive training opportunities both for those carrying out the policy, and for potential recruits and employees from the black communities, integrated where possible but separate if necessary, and focused on enabling the latter to fulfil their potential.

7 Designate an Equal Opportunities Manager who, until all departments or divisions of the company or group have EOP fully operational, shall be responsible for assisting line managers to draw up an action plan both linked to business needs and aimed at maximising the benefits of a diverse workforce, and for ensuring the policy, its monitoring and the related practices are carried through.

8 Make racial harassment and racial discrimination – verbal, non-verbal or physical – serious offences under the firm's disciplinary code, to be fully and properly investigated by a panel which includes black representation wherever possible, this information to be clearly publicised in the company's terms and conditions of employment.

9 Publish an annual employee profile by ethnic origin, gender and grade within the company as part of the Annual Report, and use this to enhance the company's image as a progressive employer.

10 Consider making one Board member responsible for oversight of EOP monitoring, and seek actively for a professionally qualified black Board member.

© *Churches Commission for Racial Justice*

Wanted: ombudsman for racial minorities

Vernon Bogdanor calls for a new approach to the intolerance that is spreading through Europe

Are ethnic minorities once again under threat in the new Europe? The resurrection of extremist parties in Austria, Belgium, France and Italy has coincided with the revival of popular nationalism in many of the new democracies of Central and Eastern Europe.

In consequence, the pressure on the civil and constitutional rights of minorities in democratic countries seems more severe than it has been at any time since 1945. This is chronicled in a new study, *Political Extremism and the Threat to Democracy in Europe.*

In modern times, racialism seems to appear in waves in Europe and to take on a transnational character. In the 1880s and 1890s, economic depression and the end of dreams of a liberal Europe gave rise, in Germany and Austria, to the birth of anti-semitic movements. In the 1930s, the depression put the Nazis in power and led to the spread of anti-semitism.

During the post-war era, stability in Europe has been a product largely of two political forces – social democracy and Christian democracy. With these ideologies in disarray, it is perhaps not surprising that racist movements should seek to fill the vacuum. In Britain in the Nineties, as in the Thirties, extremist parties have been unable to gain a foothold in democratic politics. Yet, the same forces that besmirch the Continent find their outlet in Britain in racial harassment and racial attacks.

In 1993, a report from the London Research Centre reported that about 58,000 households in the capital – one in 18 of black and ethnic minority households – had been subjected to attack. One third of these households still felt under threat. The Runnymede Trust estimates that there are 70,000 racial incidents a year – 200 a day, one every seven or eight minutes. No wonder the Trust concludes that 'racial harassment is endemic to British society'.

Many organisations concerned with race relations believe that racial violence and harassment should be defined as specific criminal offences. This, they argue, would signify society's abhorrence of racially motivated crime and offer moral support for harassed minorities. Yet to require proof of racial motivation could make it more difficult to secure convictions. A racist motive should be relevant at the sentencing stage, rather than through the creation of a new offence which, by complicating the law, would allow some of the guilty to escape.

Laws perhaps have only a limited role to play in securing better race relations. In 1944, the World Jewish Congress published details of anti-racist legislation that had been passed during the inter-war years in Austria, Czechoslovakia, France, Germany and the Netherlands. It had done little good.

The key to improving better race relations lies less in legal reforms than in altering a political culture which, while in principle committed to equality, remains insensitive to the needs and aspirations of ethnic minorities.

One powerful way to combat racism is to bring the facts of racial violence and harassment to a wider public, which can then be challenged to live up to its principles. The Commission for Racial Equality campaigns hard for better race relations, but its members are appointed by the Government and this limits what it can do. A more powerful institutional instrument is needed to complement its work.

Experience of the Ombudsman, since 1967, has shown how powerful an instrument it can be in enforcing good practice upon the institutions of government. An Ombudsman specifically appointed with responsibility for Race Relations could, if backed up by a parliamentary Select Committee, exert enormous pressure for better race relations.

Such an Ombudsman should have the power to investigate complaints against central government, the police, national public bodies, educational institutions and local authorities.

There should be direct access to the Race Relations Ombudsman, as there is to the Health Service Ombudsman, filtered perhaps through local racial equality councils, where it proves difficult to persuade victims to act for themselves. Where the recommendations of the Ombudsman are ignored, he or she would inform a Select Committee of the Commons which would call for parliamentary action. In this way, an Ombudsman for Race Relations, complementing rather than substituting for the law, could, by pressing for standards of good practice, make a very real difference to our political culture.

But, of course, responsibility for good race relations cannot be shuffled off on to an Ombudsman or any other official body. The prime responsibility lies with political leaders. For it is they who create the climate of opinion within which racial harassment appears acceptable. Racist parties have never been successful in democracies unless democratic politicians have co-operated with them. Hitler triumphed when German democrats tried to use him

> **The Runnymede Trust estimates that there are 70,000 racial incidents a year – 200 a day, one every seven or eight minutes**

for their own ends; the *Front National* in France won its first electoral breakthrough by means of an electoral pact with the Gaullist RPR, while the Italian neo-fascists have been welcomed into government by democratic parties.

Political leaders need to show, through action as well as words, their abhorrence of racialism. Surprisingly, perhaps, they have a better record on the Continent than do British counterparts. When, in 1990, a Jewish cemetery at Carpentras was desecrated, President Mitterand and other leading politicians led 100,000 protesters through Paris. In Sweden in 1992 the King led politicians in a march against racism. In Britain, too, ministers ought to visit the areas in which racial attacks occur, as they do after terrorist attacks, condemning the incidents and offering succour to the victims.

Racial attacks, however, do not occur in a vacuum. They occur within a political system in which immigration and asylum policies are based upon the assumption that people from different cultures constitute a 'problem'. It is hardly surprising then if, at the level of the streets and housing estates, members of ethnic minorities are also seen as a 'problem', against whom harassment is justified. Paddy Ashdown is one of the very few leading politicians to have perceived that good race relations are indivisible, that the cause of ethnic minorities in Britain is also the cause of Vietnamese refugees in Hong Kong and Muslim refugees in Bosnia.

Ministers should begin to emphasise the positive contribution that immigrants from the Huguenots onwards have made to both the prosperity and culture of this country. Instead of defining those from different cultures as a threat, why can they not bring themselves to welcome that diversity which is, after all, the hallmark of any truly liberal society?

● *Political Extremism and the Threat to Democracy in Europe* is published by the Institute of Jewish Affairs, 79 Wimpole St, London, W1M 7DD. Vernon Bogdanor is Reader in Government at Oxford University and a fellow of Brasenose College.

© The Independent
November, 1994

Harassment or law enforcement?

MP calls for an end to stop and search 'discrimination'

Bernie Grant MP has issued a challenge to Metropolitan Police Commissioner Sir Paul Condon to explain why almost half of all the stop and searches carried out in London are on Black people.

Grant said: 'In some parts of London, 57 per cent of all stop and search procedures are carried out on Black people. This confirms the impression most Black people have had for some time.'

By Anthony André

Among the areas to have gained notoriety for abnormally high stops are areas of high Black concentration, including Stoke Newington and Tottenham, in north London, Battersea and Brixton, in south London, and Notting Hill in north-west London.

Investigation

Black student Tony Leslie, who took part in a recent *Sunday Times* investigation into police stops, told the *Voice*: 'One night, I was driving a convertible Mercedes and was told that both I and it looked out of place in that part of north London.

Another time, I was stopped because they said that at a distance of 100 metres I looked like a wanted criminal, and the last time they claimed it was just 'routine.' It seems to me that if the constant stopping of Black people is routine, then it's a pretty bad routine.'

National figures issued last year sparked an outcry at the revelation that nearly half of all the people stopped and searched were, not surprisingly, from ethnic minorities.

Although the rules governing police stop and search changed dramatically in the mid-80s with the introduction of The Police and Criminal Evidence Act of 1984 ('PACE') – when strict guidelines demanded that police officers should have reasonable grounds for suspicion before carrying out a search – it has made little difference.

New Scotland Yard has denied abusing the stop and search laws. They said: 'We strongly refute any suggestion that the Metropolitan Police applies stop and search laws in a racially discriminatory manner.'

Condemned

But Mr Grant, sharing a platform with Andrew Puddephatt, general secretary of Liberty, the civil liberties group, condemned the police figures.

Grant said: 'Every day, somewhere in London, average Black people are being subjected to the indignity of stop and search. It is clear that Black people in particular are being singled out by the police to an extent which cannot be justified.'

Argument

Black people account for 25.5 per cent of stop and search incidents London-wide yet, according to the population census, represent only about 9 per cent of London's population – thus reinforcing the discrimination argument.

In the capital, however, it is not only the Metropolitan Police that have come in for criticism. The City of London Police has also come under fire – accused of using their highly publicised 'ring of steel' anti-terrorism security cordon to stop and search ethnic minorities.

A spokesman defended the force: 'The style of policing practised in the city includes a highly visible, pro-active uniformed presence, supplemented by advanced camera technology.'

He added that they would continue to employ such methods for prevention and detection purposes, 'in relation to all styles of criminality'.

Now both Mr Grant and Mr Puddephatt are calling on the government to suspend the implementation of further changes governing police stop and search – in the light of the new Criminal Justice Bill.

They are demanding detailed examination and research into current figures before additional police powers come into force in March of this year.

Their concern is centred around Clause 55 of the Justice Bill, which they believe will renew the right of the police to stop and search anyone on a whim, without having 'reasonable grounds'. This, they believe, will lead to increased police harassment of ethnic minorities.

The new powers will grant police the right to stop and search anyone within a specific area in which a serious crime has taken place.

Hampshire Chief Constable Hoddinott – spokesman for the Association of Chief Police Officers – argued: 'The exercise of this power will be carefully monitored – in particular regarding ethnic classification.'

Despite these reassurances, Mr Grant underlined his determination to carry the fight further, and vowed to urge shadow Home Secretary Jack Straw to pursue the argument in the House of Commons.

Grant concluded: 'If you look at these published figures, you can only imagine what the real figures are like.'

© The Voice
February, 1995

Black people more likely to be stopped by police

Black people are nearly seven times as likely as their White counterparts to be stopped and searched by police, new official figures reveal

They account for 25 per cent of all such swoops in England and Wales. In London the proportion rises to over 40 per cent.

The statistics are the first ever to give a racial breakdown of stop and search incidents.

London Labour MP Bernie Grant said the figures for the capital proved a 'massive amount of discrimination against Black Londoners by the police. Police have got it in for Black people.

The figures come just days after a Home Office report urging comprehensive ethnic monitoring of stop and search drug swoops.

The report said the tactic remained an 'essential' part of policing but claimed that racial analysis would help improve relations between police and ethnic minorities.

There were over 440,000 search incidents in the 12 months to April, last week's figures revealed, half of which took place in the capital.

© The Voice
January 1995

Whitewash

Racism and the law

Britain's far-right parties may perform miserably at elections, but its racist thugs match up to any in Europe. In recent months white gangs have stabbed or bludgeoned several Asians in London's East End. Ethnic minorities throughout Britain complain of persistent, petty, abuse. Whites, they say, spit on them and push excrement through their letter-boxes. Racist incidents recorded by the police have doubled in the past five years. The Home Office recently estimated that over 130,000 racially motivated crimes, including 32,000 assaults, take place each year.

Politicians are scrabbling to find ways of demonstrating their concern. One option to be proposed by the House of Commons Home Affairs Select Committee in a report to be published on June 22nd is to create a new offence of racially motivated violence. A murderer who is racially motivated, for example, could incur an extra five years in jail. The idea has garnered support from some MPs from both parties.

But others, including the government, are rightly concerned that such suggestions could rebound on ethnic minorities, undermining the concept of equality before the law which should be their greatest protection. Whites, for example, may understandably feel aggrieved if an attacker of whites is dealt with more softly than an attacker of blacks. In any case, judges are already allowed to increase a punishment if they detect racial motivation, a power open to the same objection. The new offence would only make the courts ponder the racial element of crimes more explicitly.

Many ethnic minority groups, however, see the debate over the new offence as an irrelevance. They reckon there is a deeper problem: the bias of the criminal justice system. 'One of the main concerns of the

Photo: David Hoffman

black community is the racism of the police themselves,' says Kevin Blowe from the Newham Monitoring Project, which helps victims of racial harassment in the East End. The police, he complains, do not make proper use of their powers to prosecute racists. Blacks who try to report racial incidents often claim that officers arrest them instead.

Certainly, ethnic minorities distrust the police. A recent poll by MORI in Merseyside showed that 75% of blacks say relations with the police are poor, compared with only 14% for whites. And Home Office research shows that blacks (though not Asians) are particularly unlikely to report crimes. The explanation given by many is that they fear or dislike the police. Ethnic minority lawyers, victims and suspects, also regularly accuse the police of abusing their stop and search powers, and accuse the courts of discriminating against blacks.

Are the police and courts really biased against ethnic minorities? Senior officers, such as Paul Whitehouse, the chief constable of Sussex, take pains to denounce police racism.

But evidence does suggest discrimination among rank-and-file officers.

Consider the claim that the police do not take racial crime seriously. The Home Office estimates from surveys of ethnic minorities that each year 50,000 racially motivated crimes are reported to the police. Yet, strangely, the police recorded only 8,700 racially motivated crimes last year. One explanation is that officers ignore the racial aspect of crimes, recording, say, a case of racial harassment as a mere neighbourhood dispute. 'The forces of the establishment don't like to have too much trouble over race,' says Sir Ivan Lawrence, the Tory chairman of the Home Affairs Select Committee.

Nobody doubts that disproportionate numbers of blacks are stopped and searched by the police. Home Office research shows they are twice as likely to be stopped as whites. The police point out that this does not prove discrimination. Blacks, for example, are more likely to live in poorer, higher-crime areas. But Herman Ouseley, chairman of the government-funded Commission for Racial Equality, says this does not explain all the discrepancy. 'A black person will be stopped just as much in Westminster as in Brixton,' he complains.

In the courts, too, research indicates bias against black suspects. A tenth of men in prison are black, nine times their proportion in the population. Partly that is because blacks are more likely than whites to be charged with crimes by the police. But it seems not to be the whole story. Roger Hood, a criminologist at Oxford University, recently compared sentencing of blacks and whites. Factors such as the seriousness of the crime and the offender's history were taken into account. Yet still, Mr Hood calculated, blacks received harsher sentences. © *The Economist June, 1994*

EU warned of growing racism

By John Carvel in Strasbourg

European union heads of government will be confronted at their summit in Essen next month with a disturbing analysis of growing racism in Europe which cannot be countered properly without changes to the Maastricht treaty.

The warning comes in the interim report of a committee of experts appointed by the Corfu summit in June on the initiative of Chancellor Helmut Kohl and President François Mitterrrand.

This was widely interpreted at the time as an attempt to shelve the subject until after the German and French elections. But the committee's hard-hitting report is likely to put the issue at the centre of political debate.

It expresses 'concern and fear' about displays of racism which are increasing in number and seriousness. 'These occurrences take the form of spontaneous or organised violence, leaving behind victims dead and injured.

'Racism and xenophobia have become commonplace not only in day-to-day neighbour disputes but also in the pronouncements of certain extremist organisations and within certain political parties,' the report says.

There was evidence of supranational racist networks whose main targets were foreigners, said the draft text prepared by the committee's chairman, Jean Kahn, head of the European section of the World Jewish Congress and a politically ally of Edouard Balladour, the French prime minister.

The recommendations – to be finalised at a meeting in Paris in the next few days – will include changes to the Maastricht treaty to give the EU clear competence to fight discrimination on grounds of race, ethnic origin or religion.

'It will make it possible to adopt European directives laying down national obligations,' the draft text says.

The proposal will be uncomfortable for heads of government who have argued that race relations are an internal matter which should not be open to European Commission interference. An EU race relations directive could establish laws to prevent discrimination in employment and housing against about 17 million EU residents and citizens whose ethnic origins lie outside the EU.

Other recommendations in the Kahn report include:

- An EU equal opportunities committee to foster good relations with minorities and ensure the removal of discrimination
- An EU equal opportunities committee to foster good relations with minorities and ensure the removal of discrimination
- A code of ethics against racism to establish principles of tolerance and equality
- Mobilisation of young people in voluntary work to promote better understanding
- A European ombudsman for national and foreign minorities
- The introduction into school curricula of teaching on human rights and non-discrimination
- The publication in each member state of a European anti-racist handbook setting out foreigners' rights and means of redress, to be widely distributed among vulnerable communities.

The report is likely to provoke heated debate about whether racism should be on the agenda for the 1996 intergovernmental conference to review the Maastricht treaty.

Glyn Ford, the European parliament's representative on the Kahn committee, said it was politically desirable to give the Union a clear right to intervene.

'But this should not be taken as an excuse for the commission failing to use its existing powers to the limit over the next two years,' Mr Ford said.

- The European Commission said yesterday that economic co-operation with the Mediterranean countries was the best way to fight terrorism, Islamic fundamentalism and uncontrolled migration.

© The Guardian
November, 1994

Photo: David Hoffman

Racism and xenophobia have become commonplace.

No room for racism

From the BBC and the Commission for Racial Equality (CRE)

For as long as anyone can remember, and for centuries before that, Britain has been home to people from many parts of the world. They came here at different times, and for all sorts of reasons:

- The Romans, Angles, Saxons, and Normans came as invaders and conquerors.
- Others came as traders, or to find work.
- Jewish and Irish people – and many others – came to escape from war, famine or religious hatred in their own countries.
- There were also those who had no choice – Africans brought to Britain by force as slaves or servants.
- People from countries such as India, Pakistan, Bangladesh, and the West Indies were invited here after the Second World War, because there were not enough people to do all the jobs.

Britain has never been a place where everyone is the same. There have always been 'ethnic minorities', people with roots in other parts of the world. In 1764, there were about 20,000 black people in London.

Today, about 3 million people in Britain call themselves 'black,' 'Asian,' or 'Chinese,' or say they belong to some other group. Nearly half of them were born and brought up here, and many of them can speak more than one language.

Throughout history, some of the people who were already settled here made it very hard for those who came later.

When Jewish people first came here more than 1,000 years ago, they had to obey all sorts of special rules. They were not allowed to set up businesses or buy land. They were made to wear a badge on their clothes – a piece of yellow material six fingers

long and three fingers broad – so that people could tell who they were. All sorts of ridiculous stories were made up about them – and people believed them. Jewish people were treated cruelly, called names, and often attacked, just because they were from a different 'race'.

Britain has never been a place where everyone is the same. There have always been 'ethnic minorities', people with roots in other parts of the world

---

When black and Asian people arrived in Britain in the 1940s, they were shocked by the rudeness and open racism towards them. There were big signs up saying black and Irish people were not allowed in pubs, and many landlords and landladies refused to rent rooms to them. Like Jewish people before, they were called names, threatened, and attacked. And all because of their 'race' or the colour of their skin.

Things like this still happen today. Why do we treat people badly just because they are different from us?

The answer is prejudice. But what does this mean?

Prejudices are opinions that we form without knowing all the facts. Most of us make up our minds about things far too quickly, and stick to our opinions even when we are wrong. What would you say if your friend told you not to live next to anyone from Birmingham, because her neighbours are too noisy, and they are from Birmingham? Or if someone says that the English are all football hooligans? We have opinions like these about everything under the sun – food, clothes, music, sport, and people.

Many of the prejudices we have don't hurt anyone. But some prejudices can be harmful, especially when people are treated unfairly because of them. Treating someone unfairly because of prejudices about their race or colour is called racial discrimination. Racial discrimination is against the law.

You have rights

If you think someone has been unfair to you or is treating you badly because of your race or colour, you have the right to tell someone about it. If it happens at school you should make a complaint to your teacher.

You have responsibilities too

You should never treat anyone badly because of their race or colour, in school or out.

Try and help anyone who is being treated unfairly or bullied because of their race or colour. Let them know that they can count on you for support.

Can anyone else help?

If you are called racist names or bullied or pushed around because of your race or colour, the most important thing is to talk to someone you trust as soon as possible. You can talk to someone in your family, a teacher whom you trust, your doctor, or another grown-up. Don't think this is telling on other children. You have rights.

The Commission for Racial Equality was set up by the Government to help get rid of racial discrimination. If you want more information about what it does, or about racism in Britain, phone or write to ask for *Without Prejudice*, which the CRE has published with BBC Radio One. The CRE can also send you a copy of *Kick It*, a new magazine about the campaign to 'kick racism out of football.'

For example:

- A school tells a Bengali family that there are no places left. Then, the next day, the family hears that a white child has got a place. Is this fair?

- A black family who go to see a flat are told that it has gone. An hour later, a white family is told that it is still for rent. Is this fair?

It's never too late to recognise our own prejudices and do something about them.

If you saw the BBC series *Dynamite*, you will know that people's prejudices sometimes get completely out of control. There are some people in Britain today who think that the colour of a person's skin, or their race, automatically makes them better or worse than others. So they taunt people about their race or colour and call them racist names, bully and threaten them, and paint racist slogans on walls. Sometimes they beat them up, and even kill them.

- Rohit Duggal, 16 years old, was stabbed to death when he went out with some friends to celebrate his GCSE results. Rohit was an Asian.

- Stephen Lawrence, 18 years old, was waiting at a bus stop with his friend when he was killed by a gang of white teenagers. Stephen was black.

- Quddus Ali, 17 years old, was chased down a street by a gang and beaten senseless. He was unconscious in hospital for four months. Quddus is an Asian.

Rohit and Stephen were killed because of the colour of their skin.

Quddus almost died because of it.

These killings took place in south London and east London. In these areas, many black and Asian people live in fear that they might be next. There are other places, too, where people feel threatened because of their race or colour. They have to think twice about doing simple, everyday things that most people take for granted – like going over to a friend's place, or walking to school, or playing in the street, or going to a football match. Even home is not completely safe from attacks. Most people are horrified by such violent crimes.

After reading about such violence and hatred, it's hard to believe that people from different ethnic groups get on much better today than they ever have in the past. But that is a fact. Many young people today, especially in big cities, have more friends from other backgrounds than their parents ever did. They have more in common because of school, clubs, music, sport and fashion. They don't let things like race or colour come between them.

People from ethnic minorities also have a better chance today of doing the kinds of jobs they want to do. Some become doctors, lawyers, scientists or musicians. Some set up their own businesses or work for other people. Others have become famous. Colin Jackson, Linford Christie and Paula Dunn Thomas are all international athletics champions. Lenny Henry is a well-known TV comedian. And there are *Blue Peter's* Diane-Louise Jordan, *Record Breakers'* Kriss Akabusi, and *Live and Kicking's* Andi Peters. Apache Indian and Des'ree are pop singers who have had chart success. Meera Sayal is now a top TV actress, and Josette Simon has made a name for herself on the stage. There are even six Asian and black MPs in Parliament today.

- This article was produced by the CRE in association with the Children's BBC/EBU (European Broadcasting Union) series, *Dynamite*.

© *Commission for Racial Equality, 1994*

Anger over UN investigation into racism in Britain

By Marianne Curphey

Plans for a three-year United Nations investigation into race relations in Britain have split equal rights campaigners and black pressure groups.

The inquiry into discrimination in the legal system, education, housing, health and unemployment has been welcomed by the Commission for Racial Equality (CRE). However, some black groups and unions doubt it will lead to improvements in race relations.

MPs also questioned the UN inquiry. Sir Ivan Lawrence, chairman of the Commons Home Affairs Select Committee, said: 'Our concern on race relations is constantly monitored and frequently investigated . . . Let the United Nations look at those countries where race relations and human rights are a disgrace.'

Winston Churchill, Conservative MP for Davyhulme, Manchester, said: 'I would have thought the UN would have had better things to do than . . . to devote a lot of attention to the United Kingdom where we have gone a long way to safeguard the rights of ethnic minorities.'

Conservative MP Dame Jill Knight said: 'We have already spent a considerable amount of time working on the Home Affairs Select Committee report on this issue and all they need to do is to read that.'

A special inspector from the UN Human Rights Commission is to be sent to Britain to study discrimination and intolerance. His investigation will be part of a wider scrutiny of developing nations' policies towards ethnic minorities.

Meetings between the inspector, Maurice Glegle-Ahanhanzo from Benin, West Africa, and Home and Foreign Office ministers were due to start last week but he cancelled at the last minute due to 'unforeseen circumstances'.

While the Government is keen to emphasise that Britain has not been singled out for special attention, the CRE believes more legislation is needed to protect black communities. Racist incidents have risen by 50 per cent during the past five years to 130,000 annually.

A special inspector from the UN Human Rights Commission is to be sent to Britain to study discrimination and intolerance

Margaret Michie, of the CRE, said: 'Although Britain has had more comprehensive race relations legislation than other European countries, we believe there is room for improvement.'

Claude Moraes, director of the Joint Council for the Welfare of Immigrants, welcomed the inquiry. 'This Government may introduce new legislation if the two reports turn out to be internationally embarrassing,' he said.

However, Makbool Javaid, chairman of the Society of Black Lawyers, said: 'You cannot fight racial discrimination by proclamation.' Bill Morris, head of the Transport and General Workers' Union, said the UN did not need 'to tell black people what we already know'.

The CRE and Equal Opportunities Commission publish today a survey that shows unemployment among ethnic minority women is 16 per cent compared with 6 per cent for white women; for ethnic minority men the figure is 20 per cent, almost double that for white men.

The UN created the post of special rapporteur on racial discrimination last year after complaints that its human rights investigations focused almost exclusively on Third World countries. Rapporteurs can condemn rights abuses, and urge condemnatory resolutions by the UN, but there are no other sanctions.

© Times Newspapers Ltd 1994

Photo: David Hoffman

Racist incidents have risen by 50 per cent during the past five years

Living with violence

An extract from *One Race*

For most black people in Britain today, the fear of violence is never far away. Not many white people know what it feels like to have insults shouted at them in the street. Pastor Laurence speaks on the *One Race* cassette tape of the shock and upset such attacks cause.

Glasgow is a city with pride in its record of hospitality to refugees, and indeed to all black people. Now black people in Glasgow speak of attacks in the public street: being called names, told to go 'home' (even though many are Scottish born and bred), derisive singing of the nursery rhyme 'Baa Baa Black Sheep,' being threatened, spat on, black children pushed out of their place in bus queues, even unprovoked hair-pulling by white adults. Black Glaswegians have found their cars vandalised and burnt, excrement pushed through the letter-box, bricks thrown through their windows. Some black households now put a bucket of water beneath the letter-box every evening before retiring, for fear of arson in the night.

'Keep on your guard...'

The fear of violence is often a big problem in itself. It can take all the pleasure out of living in the neighbourhood, even make people afraid to go out at all. 'Walking down the street, you have always to be braced for name-calling and worse. Nothing may happen for a week, but . . .'

'A lot of the time racism is a constant thing,' one woman said; 'You put up with graffiti and name-calling and vandalism and being told you're only imagining it. It only gets noticed when it's a petrol bomb through the door.' The attitude of police, black women say, has too often been 'when there's trouble you should just walk away.' One of the women's main hopes is that a Racial Violence Monitoring Group should be set up in Glasgow. They want staff who will 'listen to people without telling them they're imagining it.'

Research has shown that harassment has serious effects on health, and also on school performance. Often it's the fear and stress that does most damage. It also affects housing policy. Councils and housing associations may concentrate black tenants in one area, in a bid to reduce neighbour troubles. Then the black tenants find themselves blamed for causing all the problems by 'wanting

to live in ghettos' and 'refusing to integrate'.

Self defence?

Organising black community self-help in the face of racist violence is made more difficult by the unspoken attitude of many white people, that black people are themselves to blame for the violence because their presence provokes it, and if they campaign for the right to live in peace, that is an even bigger provocation. Black people who speak out often make themselves particular targets for racist violence. There is usually a big fuss in the press when black communities make arrangements to defend their vulnerable members from attack. Racist attacks, even on children, elderly people or pregnant women, hardly ever cause the same excitement.

White people need to understand that in a society where black people are constantly treated with hostility by total strangers who have nothing against them but their colour, you have to prove you're a friend if you don't want to be mistaken for an enemy. 'When you walk down a street full of white people,' one black Glasgow woman pointed out, 'you can't tell by sight which are the ones who'd attack you.'

● The above is an extract from *One Race*, a study pack for churches on racial violence, avaiable from Churches Commission for Racial Justice. Address details page 39.
© Churches Commission for Racial Justice

Reported race attacks double in five years

Police figures prompt calls for separate offence of harassment

Reported incidents of racial violence have increased sharply in the past year and doubled in the last five years, a new survey of police forces in England and Wales shows.

In some regions, the number of reported racial incidents, including assaults, threats and vandalism, has risen by up to 20-fold. Racist abuse has doubled since 1988 to more than 8,700 cases in 1993 – an increase of about 1,000 on the previous year.

The Labour Party, which published the official police figures yesterday, called for new laws to clamp down on racist attacks. It is urging the Government to introduce legislation to make racial harassment a separate offence.

Labour also wants racial motivation to be made a compulsory factor in cases of violence – which would force courts to give tougher sentences when proven. At present it is optional.

Labour plans to table an amendment at the report stage of the Criminal Justice Bill in the Commons. Hartley Booth, the Tory MP, unsuccessfully sought a second reading for such a measure last week.

According to statistics from 42 of the 43 police forces in England and Wales, there was a 13 per cent rise in racial incidents over the previous year. There have been dramatic increases in areas such as Greater Manchester, which rose from 28 in 1988 to 577 last year. The increase from 1992 to last year was more than 40 per cent.

The Metropolitan Police, which accounts for about 40 per cent of incidents, saw a rise from more than 3,200 cases in 1992 to an estimated 3,550 last year. The force has reported

By Jason Bennetto

a rise of nearly 300 per cent in reported racial incidents on the Isle of Dogs in east London since the election last September of a far-right British National Party councillor in a local ward.

Other forces to show sharp rises from 1992 to 1993 included Hampshire, Avon and Somerset, Essex, Derbyshire, Leicestershire and South Wales. The West Midlands, West Yorkshire and Durham have shown a decrease.

The Home Office says the number of reported incidents may have risen during the past five years because of the increased confidence and awareness among ethnic minority groups, who are now more willing to contact the police.

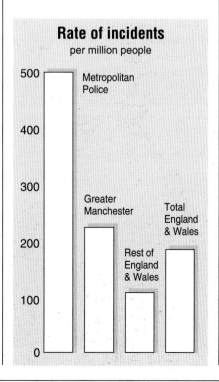

Rate of incidents
per million people

Yesterday's figures, however, still only give a snapshot of the true scale of racist abuse in Britain. Peter Lloyd, Minister of State at the Home Office, giving evidence to the Home Affairs Select Committee, which is investigating Racial Attacks and Harassment, said that there could be as many as 130,000 racial incidents every year.

The Anti-Racist Alliance estimates that in the past two years 14 people have died as a result of racial attacks; however no official figures are known because such murders are not recorded separately.

Tony Blair said: 'Given that the number of incidents reported are a tiny fraction of the actual number, there could be anywhere between 150,000 and 200,000 such incidents each year, and many of them will involve serious physical violence.'

He said tougher penalties would not be the only result: 'It would also send out a very clear signal from Parliament. We need to send out the clearest possible signal that racial violence and harassment will not be tolerated.'

Joan Ruddock, a Labour home affairs spokeswoman, yesterday called on the Government to investigate the growth in fascist parties in Britain and their link with the rise in racist incidents.

Michael Howard, the Home Secretary, has said he is prepared to consider making changes to the Public Order Act regarding racial verbal abuse and harassment, but he believes that a separate offence of racial violence would make it harder to convict someone.

© The Independent
March, 1994

Stay and stand

At what point is racial harassment seen as a priority?
Many victims suffer intimidation before any action is taken

by Angella Johnson

Racial harassment includes not only physical attacks on persons and damage to property, but also verbal abuse and any other form of behaviour which deprives people of the peaceful enjoyment of their homes on grounds of racial origin.

Ahmed and Christine (not their real names) slept with a bucket of water under the letterbox inside their flat. Another mixed-race family on their south London council estate had been fire-bombed twice and they feared they might be next. The couple, both aged 19, had suffered more than a year of verbal racial harassment and threats after moving to a two-bedroom flat on the Hillcrest estate in Lewisham. But when they requested a transfer the council refused on the grounds that theirs was not a 'last resort' situation.

So at what point is racial harassment considered a priority and therefore warranting immediate rehousing by the council? Lewisham, like many authorities, has a policy of not bowing to the pressure of bigots. 'If we moved people willy-nilly it would be like giving *carte blanche* for racists to continue harassment. We don't want to create racially segregated estates,' said spokesman Nick Fairclough.

Admirable in principle. But for the families living in fear, such policies provide cold comfort. Richard Backes, of Lewisham Racial Equality Council (LREC), says too often families are being held hostage to a general plan to keep estates multi-racial. 'They say they want to punish the perpetrators by tackling the problem head-on, but it's usually the victims who are punished by being made to stay put.'

He suggests that councils should move victims immediately on request as recommended by the Commission for Racial Equality (CRE). 'Then they will be more likely to act as witnesses. It would make it easier to take legal action against the attackers and another black family can always be moved in once the problem has been sorted and it is safe for them to do so.'

Mr Backes believes many housing officers do not take racial harassment seriously unless injury is sustained. 'The thing about racial harassment is that it is a systematic grinding down of people. They don't have to punch you to the ground for it to be distressing.'

While most councils claim they want to take action against racists, the CRE says the small number of convictions belies any claims of success with that policy. For example, no harasser has ever been evicted by Lewisham. The borough had 141 reported cases in the year up to June, 1994 – it had agreed to transfer about 32 families.

Southwark Council in south London also has a policy of not moving tenants unless absolutely necessary. 'We think it's a failure and try to avoid it if we can,' said Jim Wintour. 'Every time you move someone you are rewarding a racist. I would offer support and plead with the victims to stay and fight but it's their call.'

The council does, however, have one of the best records of aggressively tackling allegations of racial harassment. In about 81 of the 185 cases of alleged racial harassment, families were transferred last year. Ten injunctions were granted against perpetrators. 'That shows it is not incompatible to re-house people and then take legal action,' said Mr Backes.

Southwark was recently presented with an award from the CRE for its success in dealing with the problem. The approach includes issuing mobile phones, installing burglar alarms, video cameras, special anti-arson letterboxes, security doors and personal alarms. In extreme cases, it may mean escorting children to school or offering to sleep in the family home.

Against this background the CRE says it is concerned that the fears, and needs, of victims are frequently given a low priority and get lost in the bureaucracy. 'Too often they are not given any support and

Photo: David Hoffman

Should councils move victims immediately on request?

receive additional harassment once the perpetrator is aware that a complaint has been made,' said a spokeswoman.

According to official Home Office crime figures, the number of racial attacks and harassment cases reported to the police increased by about 25 per cent between 1993 and 1994. Asians tend to be preyed upon more often than people of African-Caribbean origin. The latest official British Crime Survey shows that, in 1992, 24 per cent of victims assaulted or threatened were black, compared with about 60 per cent of Asians.

Bradford, in West Yorkshire, had 46 reported harassment cases between April 1993 and 1994 – the same as the previous year. Of those, 24 were transferred compared with two perpetrators who were moved. So far none of the attackers have been taken to court, 'but there are some cases

---

The number of racial attacks and harassment cases reported to the police increased by about 25 per cent between 1993 and 1994

---

under investigation which we hope will end with prosecutions,' said spokeswoman Louise Ragan.

Although the council does offer a comprehensive support system similar to those already mentioned, they will also transfer victims immediately on request.

Ahmed and Christine did not fall into official statistics of racial harassment because they refused to complain to the police. 'We didn't want to cause trouble, so I tried being

friendly with the lads by inviting them to attend martial arts classes I was giving on the estate,' said Ahmed. When this failed – they were not interested – and the council refused to give the couple a transfer, they took their two young children and went to live with relatives in cramped accommodation.

It was then they approached Lewisham and Mr Backes advised them to take legal action. Last month, the High Court gave them leave to apply for a judicial review to overturn the refusal.

Lewisham council eventually re-housed the couple after they had been given leave, but insisted this had not affected their decision. If the High Court hearing had been successful the council may have been forced to change its policy to transfer only as a last resort.

© *The Guardian*
October, 1994

Sticks and stones may break my bones, but words . . .

Those are brave words, but they can hide a lot of pain. Words do hurt. They can come through the letter-box on a leaflet, or maybe you have seen them scrawled in haste on the wall of a corner shop. It's hard to believe sometimes that people actually mean these sorts of things, but sadly they do. Yet no-one need put up with it. Racial abuse and insults can be against the law.

Banter on the building site

Work on a building site is tough and it can be rough. At the sharp end is tunnelling. Bill Smith's job was helping to box out a new lift shaft for London Underground. He had only been in the job a couple of days when it started. The foreman called him a 'black bastard'. That was coming up to Christmas.

By Easter, Bill had lost count of the times he had heard those words. His mates on the job did nothing.

They didn't join in, but they didn't protest either.

At first Bill just kept quiet. The work was good and well paid. It wasn't worth the risk. And anyway, perhaps the guy would get fed up and stop.

But he didn't. A company manager was there one day but did nothing when the foreman shouted at him in the usual way.

For Bill that was the last straw. He told the foreman to his face to shut up. That only seemed to provoke him. So Bill went to the management. But he got no words of support. When the foreman was needling him again during a night shift there was a row and Bill was given his cards. At that point he went to the CRE to get its help. It was able to get lawyers to argue his case – you can't get legal aid for race relations cases. It was a year before Bill's case came up in an industrial tribunal – the special courts that hear employment disputes.

An industrial relations manager for the firm came along. He said he had often heard phrases like 'black bastard' on building sites. It was all just part of the banter that went on, he claimed. The tribunal's answer was short and sweet: rubbish.

Bill and his lawyers had shown that he was insulted many times, not just once, and that his firm let it go on after Bill had protested. That meant the firm was responsible – and had to pay up when it came to damages.

At first the firm tried to appeal, but it soon saw sense. Advisers were brought in and a proper equality policy started. Bill had set a ball rolling that was getting bigger and bigger . . .

● The above is an extract from *Without Prejudice*.

© *Commission for Racial Equality/BBC*
June, 1994

An everyday story of racial hatred

Across the country ethnic minorities live in fear of random violence

By Patrick Weir

It's like being in a prison. As you can see there are very few windows that you can naturally look out of. It makes for a very confined life.'

Asif is an Asian shopkeeper on a large housing estate in Derby, highlighted by the police as a 'problem area'. He has been terrorised by a teenage gang hurling bricks and bottles at his property and screaming racial abuse. For three years his home and business have been boarded up, although this hasn't deterred the gang. 'When we came here six years ago, we had minor problems,' he explains; 'Stones were thrown at the windows and there was some verbal abuse. But over the last three years the situation has definitely got worse.'

Windows in his shop and home have been broken several times and his family has endured an increasing barrage of taunts and insults. His car has been vandalised and the windows of an Asian driver's taxi smashed with baseball bats. Drunken youths hanging around outside the shop have intimidated customers. All such incidents have been reported to the police.

The latest, and potentially most dangerous, incident occurred a few weeks ago. 'During the day those youths had been throwing stones at the shop,' says Asif; 'I told them to go away, and they just insulted me. I contacted the police and they said they'd send a car round immediately. Nobody came, so I telephoned again but was told it wasn't an emergency.' By now the gang had gone, but half an hour later they returned.

Asif was comforting his frightened, 11-year-old asthmatic son when the brick hit the window. 'I could have been killed,' he says, as he draws back the curtain to show the shattered glass; 'The fact that it was double glazed save my life.' For the first time the police were able to act. Having recognised some of the youths earlier that day, Asif provided names and descriptions and six members of the gang were arrested. 'In the past I've not been able to identify anyone as they congregated in groups at night,' he says. 'However, not all the gang have been caught. The problem is still under investigation and my family is still frightened. It is creating a lot of pressure and we feel very uneasy.'

As do the residents of the estate, none of whom has dared to give a statement to the police for fear of retribution. As frustrated as he is, Asif understands this fear. 'People don't want to come to any harm themselves and I sympathise with them. But the situation has become so stressful that someone has to speak out. Thankfully the police are at last doing something because they've been very slow to act in the past.

'I've rung so many times and asked them to come but they'd always arrive too late. The youths had long gone and the officers said there was nothing they could do. The strain on my wife and three children is tremendous. They can't even walk alone around here in case they are picked on.'

Leading the police investigation is WPC Kim Davison. 'When I first visited the shop I thought it was closed down,' she says; 'At night it looks like an abandoned building. To have to live like this is intolerable. When I met Asif's wife she was in tears and felt she wasn't being helped.

'It has reached the stage where they are living in constant fear, and this fear is very real. Its not just about the damage done to their home, but more the feeling that they are being

made to suffer. Their shop has been targeted simply because they are Asian. Other shops owned by white people on the estate have suffered no problems at all.'

Catching members of the gang has proved conspicuously difficult, but Davison expects to make further arrests. 'Asif was able to identify some of the offenders and actually gave us names. He'd had suspicions as to who was involved but these weren't enough. However, we will be conducting more interviews and talking to as many people on the estate as possible. But it isn't easy.

It has reached the stage where they are living in constant fear, and this fear is very real

---

'People won't give us their name or come to court. They will tell you what they've seen off the record but daren't make statements. They are simply too scared. I've met residents who saw exactly what happened regarding the last incident. I tried to persuade them that it was sensible to give us statements but they were genuinely too frightened. It's shocking that they feel such fear. I can't believe it.'

'It's not just a case of stopping these youths but of changing their attitudes. They must learn that living in a boarded-up house and not being able to see through the windows is intolerable.'

As confused as he is angry, Asif is determined to stand his ground. 'My customers are very nice people and I feel loyal to them,' he says. 'They are aware of the problem and are very understanding. I also feel annoyed and will not be forced out. Why should these people remove us from this area? Why do they want to?'

Has he ever been tempted to take the law into his own hands? 'Yes I've been very tempted indeed, but I'm a law-abiding citizen. Anyway, if I had done anything the police would be more interested in arresting me than the real culprits.'

Leaving his house, Asif shows me his garden. It resembles waste land, the rubbish and patches of grass sadly not out of place with the desolate fortress that passes for his home. 'I can't even tend to my garden because the fences are constantly being pulled down. I've tried but what is the point?'
© *The Guardian*
July, 1994

Racist violence

Home Secretary opposes demand for new law on racist violence

A conference, 'The Future of Multi-Ethnic Britain' at Reading University, organised by the Runnymede Trust in partnership with the Commission for Racial Equality, the European Commission and the All-Party Group on Race and Community, discussed, among other matters, the electoral threat of extreme right-wing racist groups.

Trevor Phillips, a TV presenter, who is also the chairman of the Runnymede Trust, said: 'Britain has yet to come to terms fully with the social and economic necessity to establish systems and institutions which guarantee racial equality and justice.' Of the TV industry Phillips had this lament on behalf of a tiny elite including himself; 'TV thinks of itself as modern, meritocratic and a mirror of the nation. Yet it is just as exclusive as the rest of British industry and government. Ironically, all four of the non-white executives in the industry started in the same place – making minority programmes for London Weekend in the early eighties. It is a damning indictment that in more than a decade we have not moved on.' Phillips, of course, failed to deal with the wider issue of 'apartheid in the media' which keeps out young talented, black people, often with the connivance of some 'Asian and black tokens' who are even more frightened of able black and Asian talent than their white colonial bosses. These misled 'tokens' see such people as a threat to their own jobs.

Michael Howard, the Home Secretary, told the conference: 'We cannot afford to be complacent and must retain a strong framework of law and clearly stated policies.' But he disagreed with those calling for specific legislation to tackle racial violence and harassment. 'The fundamental fact is that all acts of violence are already criminal offences... Courts can and do take racial motivation into account as an aggravating factor when passing sentence.'

Herman Ouseley, chairman of the Commission for Racial Equality (CRE), hoped that all citizens 'equally recognise and accept multi-ethnic Britain as a positive feature of the heritage and fabric of their society, whether they are black, white, Asian, old or young, live in a multi-ethnic area or not.'

The CRE chairman also criticised some sections of the media citing the example of the wide publicity given to the killing of a white young man while racially motivated killings of black people are given relatively low coverage.

Ouseley also called for the strengthening of the existing anti-discrimination laws and tougher new laws to help the CRE in its fight against racial discrimination and racially motivated violence.
© *The Asian Times*
October, 1994

A campaign

Where's the racism in football? Was a campaign really necessary? Won't the problem just get worse if it gets publicity?

The questions came thick and fast when the Kick Racism out of Football campaign was launched by the CRE and the PFA.

But we also got tremendous support from fans, fanzine writers, club officials, and others, like AH, who had this to say:

'As far as I am concerned, racism is the biggest blight on football today, and whilst I feel it has improved over the last few years (because people have grown sick and tired of this mind-numbing idiocy, and are not going to accept it anymore). I also feel that the CRE campaign will help to give the momentum needed to continue this improving trend.'

Racism in football takes many forms. There's the unmistakable racism of the vicious abuse, chanting, and pelting that black players are often greeted with when they walk onto the pitch. Such behaviour was made illegal by the Football (Offences) Act in 1991. The worst of this abuse comes from a small section of the crowd, but many players also have to put up with it from other players.

It's not only black players who have to endure this abuse; black and Asian fans are automatically included in any racist hostility. It is hardly surprising then that there are so few black supporters, when fear and apprehension are part and parcel of a day's outing to support their team. There is another type of racism that is more subtle. A quick count of the people from ethnic minorities in football clubs and in the football establishment says it all – at one stage in 1993/94, 2 team managers out of 92 football clubs were black; today, at the start of the 94/95 season,

there are none. There are no club chairmen from ethnic minorities either, and hardly any board members. According to the 1991 census, about 5.5% of the British population are from ethnic minorities.

Racism in football takes many forms

Things are changing, though. Professional footballers, about 20% of whom are black, often become club officials when they retire from the game, or go on to work for football authorities. It is just a matter of time therefore before they are better represented in the running of the game.

This does not, of course, explain why there are virtually no professional Asian players, even though hundreds of Asians play amateur football.

The CRE-PFA campaign was certainly not the first campaign against racism in football. There have been many others, mostly led by fans. But this is the first one to win support from all the football authorities and nearly all the professional clubs. Wimbledon striker John Fashanu, Chelsea's Paul Elliot, and Tottenham's Erik Thorsvedt were among the players who lent their weight to the campaign.

At the time of the launch over three quarters of the professional clubs in England and Wales had agreed to put posters up around their grounds and to print a statement in their programmes. The statement, co-signed by CRE chairman Herman Ouseley, and the head of the PFA, Gordon Taylor, denounces both those who are responsible for racist behaviour at football grounds and those who condone it by saying and doing nothing about it. By January 1994, all but one of the professional clubs had publicly endorsed the campaign, and many had started to take anti-racist initiatives of their own.

Posters and public statements are just the start of any serious programme to fight racism. The main aim of the campaign was to get clubs to act on a 9-point action plan. The PFA, the FA, the FA Premier League, and the Endsleigh League all joined the CRE in persuading clubs to take action.

But clubs can only do so much to rid football of racism. All the different groups involved with football owe it to the game to do their bit as well – the police, local authorities with grounds in their areas, fans, trainers, etc.

By January 1994, all but one of the professional clubs had publicly endorsed the campaign, and many had started to take anti-racist initiatives of their own.

The Football in the Community scheme, with a development officer at almost every club, stresses 'fair play' when training young people, and discourages anti-social behaviour at the grounds. It also encourages local people to get involved in the club, by organising open days and inviting players to meet them.

The future of this campaign, and others like it, depends on all those groups – and on you.

The Scottish campaign

The campaign in Scotland was launched in January 1994. Counter-signed by the Scottish PFA, the message encouraged fans and clubs to act against discrimination and harassment. The Association of Chief Police Officers in Scotland, and the Scottish FA and League, as well as over half the clubs, and many players, joined together to support the campaign.

● The above is an extract from *Kick it! The CRE/PFA Football Trust Campaign*.

© *Commission for Racial Equality 1994*

A 9-point action plan for football clubs

Clubs should take the following steps to tackle racist behaviour at football grounds:

1. Issue a statement saying that the club will not tolerate racism, and spelling out the action it will take against supporters who are caught in 'indecent or racialist chanting'. The statement should be printed in all match programmes, and displayed permanently and prominently around the grounds.
2. Make public announcements condemning any racist chanting at matches, and warning supporters that the club will not hesitate to take action.
3. Make it a condition for season-ticket holders that they do not take part in racist chanting or any other offensive behaviour, such as throwing missiles onto the pitch.
4. Take action to prevent the sale or distribution of racist literature in and around the ground on match days.
5. Take disciplinary action against players who shout racist abuse at players during matches.
6. Contact other clubs to make sure that they understand the club's policy on racism.
7. Make sure that stewards and the police have a common strategy for removing or dealing with supporters who are breaking the law on football offences. If it is dangerous or unwise to take action against offenders during the match, they should be identified and barred from all further matches.
8. Remove all racist graffiti from grounds as a matter of urgency.
9. Adopt an equal opportunities policy in the areas of employment and service provision. The Department of Employment has produced a very useful 10-point plan on equal opportunities.

Incidents of racial attacks and violence in Britain*

Year	1988	1989	1990	1991	1992
Bedfordshire	21	25	33	n/a	57
Cheshire	0	0	0	3	29
Derbyshire	17	20	53	143	60
Essex	2	26	43	59	80
Gloucestershire	17	20	51	25	33
Greater Manchester	28	40	123	204	401
Gwent	1	4	5	12	31
Hertfordshire	49	49	51	nla	106
Lancashire	75	93	201	119	231
Leicester	84	90	287	369	338
Merseyside	136	123	144	162	134
Northamptonshire	n/a	72	66	60	120
Nottingham	4	27	135	221	222
South Yorkshire	n/a	52	117	124	151
Surrey	13	7	7	50	61
West Mercia	0	6	13	3	19
West Midlands	382	169	268	445	379
West Yorkshire	386	306	254	322	218
Metropolitan Police	2214	2697	2908	3373	3227

* Source: Extracts from *Reported Racial Incidents*, Home Affairs Committee, April, 1993

Scotland the intolerable

Many believe that Scotland is free of the racial violence so common elsewhere. Deedee Cuddihy spoke to some people whose experiences jar with this perception

Scotland racist? Well, we know the English are racists – but the Scots? The people who can go abroad and not look down their noses (unlike some we could mention) at the 'foreigners' they find themselves among? The nation which, despite the xenophobic tendencies of its southern neighbour, has always put out the welcome mat for others, whatever their colour or culture?

Or so it is popularly believed. Surely the black American politician Jesse Jackson doesn't include Scotland when he speaks about racism in Britain. The sad truth is that while Scotland has never seen a race riot, never had an apartheid system, and still boasts, in Glasgow, the first public place in Britain to be named after the now South African President, Nelson Mandela, acts of racism, both large and small, are taking place here on a daily basis.

Strathclyde Regional Councillor Neelam Bakshi makes the point that it is not the black people in Scotland who cause our colour problems, it is the whites. 'Scotland has a multi-ethnic society,' she said, 'and there's no going back on that now, so the sooner we prepare our children, at home and in school, for life in a multicultural environment, the less racism there will be.'

Derek Goh, an officer with Strathclyde Community Relations Council, said that in the past six months he and his colleagues had drawn up reports on 173 cases of alleged racial harassment or discrimination.

'And you have to assume,' he added, 'that this is just the tip of the iceberg. An increasing number of people, including the Chinese, are making complaints to us about racial abuse, but we can't say for sure whether this is because racism is on the increase in Scotland or because more people on the receiving end of it are deciding to speak up.

'One of the most distressing cases we've had to deal with recently concerned a child who was so traumatised by racial abuse that every day when he came home from school, he'd rush to the bathroom and rub talcum powder on his face to make his skin look whiter.'

Harder to deal with are racist remarks of a sexually threatening nature

---

That's a story which would strike a chord with Asha, a 20-year-old university student from Glasgow, who remembers crying as a small child because she wasn't white and being told by a disgusted cousin to 'go and put Nivea cream on your face.'

She recalls an earlier incident when a shopping trip to town was cancelled because the British National Party was holding a rally. 'When my parents, who are Indian, explained to me that the BNP didn't like coloured people,' she said, 'I replied: "But they don't know me. How can they dislike me?"

'My young niece is already experiencing racism. She came back from nursery one day and said to my mother: "Granny, I don't like Indians – they're greasy".'

These days, Asha is disinclined to ignore apparently unintentional racist remarks made by white friends and acquaintances. She said: 'I just won't let them get away with saying things like Paki shop or Chinky carryout. I absolutely hate terms like that. They're pejorative and there's no disguising the fact.'

Harder to deal with are racist remarks of a sexually threatening nature which Asha has experienced in recent months while visiting white friends in an area where few Asian people live. 'On one occasion a man came up to me and said: "I've always wanted to ride a black woman," and

in a further incident another complete stranger said: "I'd love to f*** a gorgeous Paki."

'In pubs, men will come out with statements like "I find Indian women really gorgeous," as if it's a compliment. In fact, I don't find their remarks the least bit flattering.'

Asha highlighted the unpredictability of racial abuse. Most of its victims agreed that you can never be sure when and where it will strike – or who the perpetrators will be.

One male acquaintance, who is white, said he was astonished at the racist insults an African friend attracted when they walked down a busy city street together one Saturday afternoon. During their 15-minute stroll, ordinary-looking men in their late twenties, walking alone, said, in two separate incidents: 'Get back to your own country,' and 'Black

An increasing number of people, including the Chinese, are making complaints to us about racial abuse

bastard,' loudly enough for others passing by to hear.

Roti, a 13 year old African boy, who has lived in Scotland most of his life, said his first encounter with racism came when he was returning home from primary school one day and a man leaned out the window of a passing car and made a remark about his skin colour.

'I wasn't upset,' he recalled; 'Even then I knew that, throughout my life, I could expect people to say things like that from time to time.'

Depac, a 20-something musician from Glasgow, does get upset. Occasionally he responds aggressively, like the time a bus driver kept pulling away from the kerb when he and his father were trying to get on, then made a racist remark as they were paying their fares. 'I couldn't let him treat my father that way,' he said, 'so I told him to shut up or step outside for a fight – and he did shut up.'

But when Depac decided to do some Christmas shopping in Clydebank last month, and a teenager standing with a group of mates told him to 'Go home,' he said: 'I just laughed it off. He was looking for trouble and I didn't want to give him that satisfaction.'

© *The Herald (Glasgow)*
January, 1995

Flames of hate

No-one knows exactly how many racial attacks take place each year in Britain. That people are killed simply because of the colour of their skin is something most people find very hard to understand. Police figures have only been kept for the last six years but a new government survey says that there could be as many as 32,250 racial attacks on black and Asian people each year. That's as many as one every 15 minutes.

A silent street, a moonlit night, the quiet broken only by a sudden whoosh as flames leap up the front door of a suburban home. Momena and her parents were asleep upstairs when the smoke alarm first went off.

At school that term the fire fighters had been round for the summer fete. They brought their high rise platform and their hoses. Her class had done a project on fire safety. But her parents had already fitted smoke alarms. We just think it's sensible, they had told her.

When Momena was doing her project they had sat round the table one day. Mum and Dad had it all worked out. They helped her write the page on 'what to do if'. Momena got a 'Congratulations! Well done!' from her teacher and her project was displayed in the school hall on parents' evening.

When she woke up to the piercing pips of the alarm, she knew what to do. Don't panic, keep low down, close the doors, make sure everyone else is awake. Just as she had written in her project folder.

The smell was horrible – and along with the noise of the alarms was Ravi barking away with real terror in his voice. Smoke was already curling around on the landing ceiling when she managed to wake her mum and dad. They got into the back

That people are killed simply because of the colour of their skin is something most people find very hard to understand

spare room, closed the door and were just getting ready to climb out of the window onto the shed roof when there was a terrific crash and the front door was smashed in. A passing taxi driver had called up the fire brigade on the cab radio. The police came soon after.

The street was alive with flashing lights, hose reels and cups of tea. Mrs Smith, who had never even said 'Hullo' for all the time that they had lived there, brought them into her front room.

A detective came in and asked who had been the first awake? Had Momena heard anything? Any voices? 'You see,' the detective said, turning to her parents and going quiet, 'you were right, it was lighter fuel sprayed through the letter box.'

The police wanted to know why her parents had taken precautions. Had anyone threatened them? Did they suspect anyone? No, said her father, no one in particular...

● The above is an extract from *Without prejudice*.

© *Commission for Racial Equality/BBC*
June, 1994

Racism won't affect our goals

Young blacks are neither angry nor alienated – as long as they avoid the police

By Alister Morgan

It's a cold, wet Thursday night in Brixton, south London, and the Accra Football Club are training. About 20 black youths sprint around a small track in tight formation while a tall man in a woolly hat shouts encouragement. Faces contorted, the young men run through the rain, hot breath leaving smoky trails behind them. They are an imposing sight. Everyone else on the small Astroturf pitch watches jealously.

They are young, black and confident. Well, that's how they look from the outside. Yet, standing in the soft drizzle, I wonder if, like me, they ever feel a conflict between their lives in England and the Afro-Caribbean influence of their parents.

So I ask. The answer seems to be no. 'I'm influenced by my parents' background but I would say that I'm English. I've lived all my life here,' says 23 year old Jonel. Although they empathise with their parents' experience, most of them feel life has changed significantly. They describe England as their home. 'I consider myself English because my influences are English,' says 20 year old Patrick, reflecting an outlook held by the majority of the 30 young black men and women I spoke to. 'I couldn't survive back in the West Indies; this is my London, my streets . . . I know how to survive here,' 20 year old Marlon agrees.

Young blacks have inherited from their parents a keen sense of optimism and a strong desire to succeed. They worry about racism, but reject the idea that they are less likely to succeed because of the colour of their skin. 'You can't let racism affect your goals,' argues 17 year old Claudia, who is studying for her A-levels and wants to become a lawyer, 'I'm just like everyone else, with the same opportunities. I want success. You can't tell me that I won't succeed because I'm black or because I'm a female . . . times have changed and so have black women. I want to become a lawyer and I don't see any reason why that shouldn't happen.'

The boys from Accra FC feel equally certain. They believe they have the same opportunities as their white peers. They're up on the importance of a good education. Ask how they want to earn a living and few say 'professional footballer'. Instead they toss back a string of different professions: osteopath, physiotherapist, solicitor.

Statistics suggest that they will find life in the job market harder than they imagine. People of Afro-Caribbean or African origin make up 1.6 per cent of the population yet, according to Terence Braithwaite, a lecturer at the University of Coventry, graduate unemployment for ethnic minorities stands at 14 per cent – the figure for whites is 5 per cent. Moreover, a comparison by the Equal Opportunities Commission (EOC) of 16 to 24 year olds in 1993 across different ethnic groups shows that blacks are less likely to be in full employment than whites. A Labour Force survey made public last week showed that in London the unemployment rate for black males aged 16-24 currently stands at a staggering 62 per cent.

If there is a young black male who cannot relay a single story of racial discrimination, then he definitely knows a man who can. They shake their heads in disbelief at the enduring stereotypes – 'Whites talking about black kids mugging' and then the back-pedalling: 'We don't mean you, you're OK but . . .'

One of the men recalls asking a steward directions to a football match. 'You better find your way back to Heathrow Airport,' the steward replied.

We laugh and joke as we swap stories: those who have abused us at one time or another have almost

Photo: David Hoffman

become figures of fun. But the jovial atmosphere quickly dissipates as talk turns to the police. No one doubts that police treatment exposes the major differences between how black and white youths are treated in Britain. 'Too many of them have it in for blacks,' 21 year old Darren charges. 'They don't say it outright but you can see it in their eyes.' 'There are some good ones, but there are still too many racists,' 19 year old Stanley adds. 'They still have that 'slave' mentality.'

For many young black men, this position is bewildering: the police force claims to be actively recruiting from ethnic minorities and yet seems to alienate them on the streets. 'We act aggressively to get respect,' argues Marlon. 'You have to show that you're not intimidated. When there's pride at stake you don't want to lose face.'

Few of the young black men and women I spoke to could imagine their differences with the police ever being reconciled Lisa, 17, from Wembley is typical: 'It's just a case of them versus us. They don't care about black people or their rights. You only get fair treatment if you're white.' Yet 22 year old Joanne lives in London and has just completed her training to become a police officer. For her, joining up is an active stance against discrimination. 'I understand the feelings that most black people have for the police. I've shared their experiences. But I want to do something about it, to change preconceptions, and I believe the best way

to do this is from within the force.'

Ralph Braithwaite helps to run Accra FC. He believes that social institutions like the football club help to prepare young black men for the difficulties they will encounter. 'A lot of them lack discipline. Here they learn about respect for themselves,' he says; 'As black kids it will be harder for them to succeed than they think. We try to bring out their confidence so it can be applied to all walks of life. Some of them have deeper problems at home but they can find expression through sport.'

Although young black men and women belong to a sub-culture of their own – manifested in the music they listen to, the clothes they wear and the attitudes they espouse – the young blacks I spoke to identify more strongly with the broader sub-culture of urban youth. They are more likely

to be influenced by London than Georgetown in the West Indies. They support England in sport and, more important, would represent England before any other country. They feel uninhibited, assimilated and English. They also feel that the sky is the limit, that tomorrow holds promise.

Still, one question continues to nag: why do they support the English football team, yet back the West Indies when they play England at cricket? Everyone laughs. 'It's good to see black men doing well,' Patrick grins. When the England cricket team has as many black players as the national football team I suspect that they may change their minds. Until then, Norman Tebbit will have to wait a while longer.

© *The Independent*
January, 1995

Britons are born …
and born white

So says spokesman for the British National Party, Michael Newlands. Young *Guardian* writers wondered whether they should give publicity to his views at all, but then decided they should say how they felt.

How would newspapers look if they were written by children? The following report was produced for the *Guardian* by children aged between 8 and 18 from state schools in inner London. They were assisted by four American teenagers from the Children's Express New York bureau.

What if you were born in this country, lived here your entire life, and then somebody told you that you weren't really British because your skin was the wrong colour? The BNP is saying just that, and even suggesting that anyone who isn't 'undeniably British' should leave the country altogether.

We were ourselves of various races. We all stood there in his dark cramped office, with our faces burning. We didn't expect him to be

so openly racist, and just couldn't believe that he would tell us to move away when most of us were born in this country, even if our parents might have been immigrants.

Newlands kept talking about the past and how great everything was in this country in the fifties. He sounded like he'd come out of the Dark Ages. He had to revert to the past whenever we asked him a question. We think he is hiding in the past.

Q Why do you claim to be a 100% racist party? Fatima Ali, 10.

A Well, we are a racist party. The point is that experience has shown us that to try and create societies with different races, with different cultures, simply doesn't work. People don't like it.

Q If you were to repatriate black people and they were of mixed race, would you be prepared to separate families? Grace Udoh, 12.

A Well, each case would have to be looked at individually at the time.

Q If you were to repatriate Jews, where would you send them?

A Well, our policy on Jews is that they must make up their own minds, whether they're British or not.

Q What do you think about mixed marriages of black people and white, or Jews and white people?

A Well, broadly it's a mistake.
© *The Guardian*
October, 1994

Dealing with hate

Disturbing cases of racially motivated attacks are regularly hitting the headlines. Yinka Sunmonu talks to one London borough which is trying to make a difference

With the sharp rise in racially motivated harassment and attacks on black families, the London Borough of Waltham Forest is the first council to introduce a charter to combat racial harassment.[1] It was produced in response to research the council conducted in 1988 on the extent of racial harassment[2], which showed that victims reporting racial harassment often feel that local authorities are indifferent to their needs or just go through the motions without taking the matter further.

Targeted at those who live or work in the borough, the 26-page charter is divided into four parts: harassment around the home, harassment in any club or sports amenity, harassment in and around schools and colleges, and harassment on the streets and in public places. The council pledges it 'will use its powers to ensure that the perpetrators of racial attacks are prosecuted for their crimes and that these prosecutions are widely publicised'.

Waltham Forest social services department has revised its policy and procedures to make way for the promised changes. Devora Wolfson, equality unit manager, and Caron Kelly, equality officer, explained that racial harassment was one of the priority categories for the assessment and provision of services for adults and children.

Under the Children Act, social workers have a duty to provide services which take into account children's culture, race, and language. Staff must also ensure a child's safety, which includes protecting them from racial harassment. The charter recommends that perpetrators under 17 who are known to their victims should be reported to social services, as Waltham Forest's youth justice service offers a diversion scheme to keep children out of the courts.

Under the Children Act, social workers have a duty to provide services which take into account children's culture, race, and language

---

It will be part of established practice to 'seriously challenge racist attitudes and behaviour. And the young perpetrator's actions will be discussed with them in groups and individually,' said Wolfson. Practitioners will have to write pre-sentencing reports with details of previous incidents of racial harassment. This would then be considered by the court before passing sentence.

Racial harassment and its effects on black families form another area of concern. The department's policy has been revised to give staff clearer guidelines on how to tackle the problem. Training for implementing the charter will start in September. It will cover sessions on understanding the effects of racial harassment, case studies and suggestions for good practice. Staff will also learn how to carry out effective referrals and evidence gathering.

Wolfson and Kelly see the new policy and charter as positive steps to give confidence to the black and Asian communities as 'the charter shows that we are actually taking victims' concerns on board'.

But will it support black and Asian people in practice? Daniella, a 24 year old mother who lives in Leytonstone, has been racially harassed for more than three years. Her child has been spat at and she has been verbally abused and threatened with assault. After the charter was explained to her, Daniella welcomed its principles. 'I'd give it a go as I've got nothing to lose after all this time.'

However, another resident, Nene, feels that no one is listening.

Excrement has been smeared on her letterbox, her car has been vandalised and her children left scared. 'What can a charter do?' she asked; 'They need to listen to us to understand what we are going through.'

Wolfson and Kelly acknowledged that, in practice, the council will have to convince people who are suspicious about the charter.

The SSD aims to provide support to victims and their families by providing packages of care or referring them to voluntary agencies. 'We will be looking to provides support according to individual need and we will liaise with Project Against Racial Harassment and local victim support groups,' said Kelly.

Additional social work support can also be provided through hospital social workers, the housing department's social work team, and the emergency duty team which provide an out of hours service. As part of the new policy, victims will be given a copy of the racial harassment form – a record of agreement – which will outline the action to be taken, the officer's name and an agreed timescale for action.

Racial attacks and incidents

The British Crime Survey looked at how many crimes people suffered in 1988 and 1992. For racially motivated crimes against Afro-Caribbeans and Asians it gave broad estimates which showed:

- No evidence of any increase between the two surveys
- In 1992, 130,000 crimes were committed against them involving some racial element; of these 89,000 were committed against Asians and 41,000 against Afro-Caribbeans.

The survey estimates that there were roughly:

32,250 racially motivated assaults against Afro-Caribbean and Asian people in a year.

26,000 acts of vandalism

52,800 threats.

- These figures exclude the vast majority of lower level harassment cases.

© CRE Annual Report 1993

The local community will be consulted about the policy in the summer, following a process of consultation and approval by the social services committee. It will then be available in various languages, on audio cassette and in Braille.

A programme of outreach work will be undertaken to show the community what the department can offer. There will also be promotional work to draw the local community's attention to the charter. Despite the sceptical reactions of people like Nene, both Wolfson and Kelly believe that the reputation of social services can change and that given time, people will have confidence in the service provided by the SSD to those experiencing racial harassment.

[1] London Borough of Waltham Forest, *Charter on Dealing with Racial Incidents – A Safer Place to Live*, Waltham Forest Council, 1994. £3.50.

[2] London Borough of Waltham Forest, *Beneath the Surface*, Waltham Forest Council, 1990.

© Community Care
June, 1994

Racism in rural England

Report have found evidence of racial harassment in rural England. Ethnic minorities in rural communities face isolation, ignorance, and harassment, according to a report on racism in Norfolk published yesterday.

The Norwich and Norfolk Racial Equality Council found stereotyped racist attitudes in schools and workplaces, with many white people believing racism was not a problem in the county.

The survey was based on interviews with nearly 70 black people as well as questionnaires sent to 159 Norfolk organisations.

By Paul Myers

Ethnic minorities formed 1 per cent of the county's 742,000 population, and their communities were scattered throughout Norfolk.

'Racism is a problem associated in the popular imagination with inner cities,' the report says; 'The media stereotype tells us that black people are concentrated in poor quality jobs and in poor quality housing, threatening the traditional way of life and livelihood of the white indigenous population. In Norfolk this does not exist.

'Those black or Asian people that white people do meet are encountered individually and therefore constitute no real threat.'

But the ethnic community experienced harassment and hostility from neighbours on housing estates and marginalisation at work, where they were often subjected to offensive remarks. Specialist legal and counselling services should be created for ethnic minorities, and interpreting and translating services should be developed for people who spoke English as a second language.

© The Guardian
December, 1994

Racist violence must be ended

Racial violence has claimed yet another life, this time in South Wales. After a year of wide debate and deep concern, it is time to turn words into action on this social menace.

Mohan Singh Kullah, a shop-keeper in the South Wales town of Neath, died on 6 December after a fortnight on a life support machine.

His shop had been attacked on several occasions and racist abuse used against his family. Hearing yet another attack in the early hours, he went out to investigate and was battered with a brick. Three local men have been charged with his murder.

Mohan Singh died two days after a life sentence was imposed on the killer of Sudanese refugee Ali Ibrahim, murdered in Brighton in 1993. It was recommended he serve at least 20 years in view of his racist motivation.

Last year saw wide public debate around racial harassment and violence. Parliament rejected proposals for new specific offences, but did widen that of harassment.

Home Office Minister Nicholas Baker told MPs the Government 'will watch to see precisely what the new offence achieves'.

There have been commitments to further action by Government and several local authorities, particularly in pursuing a multi-agency approach. There have also been some valuable new steps, as in Burton-on-Trent where attacks can be reported to the police via local mosques or Sikh gurdwaras, but research on the ground continues to show the problem is far larger than yet grasped

> *Parliament rejected proposals for new specific offences, but did widen that of harassment*

by official policy anywhere.

A recent report on rural racism, *Not in Norfolk: Tackling the invisibility of racism*, found 'racist attitudes and behaviour are widespread and have been experienced to some degree by almost all people from ethnic minorities'. And a new study of one Leicester housing estate revealed eight out of ten ethnic minority households had experienced racial harassment during the previous two years.

As a Home Office statement said in October: 'The systematic victimisation of people because of their colour or culture is a threat to the stability and well being of a civilised society.' The statement accepted that 'the number of racially motivated incidents must have risen'.

During 1995 the CRE will seek to ensure that multi-agency approaches are in place throughout the country so that all agencies take up the responsibility they have for tackling this menace.

© Connections
January, 1995

Statistics on racial incidents

Statistics on racial incidents reported to local police forces in England and Wales are now collated by the Home Office on the basis of the financial year. The first series was published on 24 June in a Commons written reply. For April 1993 to March 1994 it gave:

Avon, Somerset	159
Bedfordshire	60
Cambridge	100
Cheshire	98
City of London	1
Cleveland	50
Cumbria	17
Derbyshire	221
Devon, Cornwall	14
Dorset	25
Durham	32
Dyfed-Powys	0
Essex	133
Gloucestershire	28
Greater Manchester	658
Gwent	21
Hampshire	212
Hertfordshire	117
Humberside	79
Kent	160
Lancashire	262
Leicestershire	315
Lincolnshire	4
Merseyside	155
Norfolk	33
North Wales	2
North Yorkshire	22
Northamptonshire	102
Northumbria	405
Nottinghamshire	264
South Wales	400
South Yorkshire	106
Staffordshire	117
Suffolk	73
Surrey	79
Sussex	214
Thames Valley	166
Warwickshire	87
West Mercia	100
West Midlands	487
West Yorkshire	244
Wiltshire	51
Provincial total	5,873
Metropolitan	3,889
TOTAL	**9,762**

© CRE
Summer, 1994

MEP demands ban on fascists

Anti-racist rally hears call for Europe-wide action

Fascist parties should be banned across the European Union, Pauline Green the leader of the socialist group of MEPs told anti-racists at the weekend.

Six years of working in a parliament where they were allowed to take their seats had convinced her of the need, she said.

Ms Green brought greetings from the European parliament's 221 strong socialist group to the National Assembly Against Racism in London's Bethnal Green.

She said that it was the right time and the right place for such a meeting, coming 50 years after the Soviet army's liberation of the Auschwitz death camp and in a place where racism was becoming 'more open and aggressive.'

She told the packed York Hall in Tower Hamlets that the socialist group, communists, greens and radicals had formed a broad alliance against the fascists in the European parliament.

They were demanding a European Union-wide race relations law to help protect the 10 million people in the EU under the most direct threat from racists and fascists.

Almost 700 people from trade unions, anti-racist and anti-fascist organisations, political parties, church groups and community defence campaigns attended the day-long conference, which launched a charter against racism.

Kumar Murshid, chairman of Tower Hamlets Anti-Racist Committee, which helped organise the Morning Star sponsored event, said that the charter would provide a way of moving the anti-racist struggle forward and into the mainstream of British politics.

Mr Murshid, a former national secretary of the Anti-Racist Alliance who resigned amid acrimoney, said that the assembly could never be 'a super-umbrella organisation to solve everything.'

He urged people to go back to their organisations and debate the charter, not as a mere form of words but as the basis for unity in action.

Left MP Ken Livingstone, a former chairman of the ARA before being voted out of office at its special annual general meeting last year, said that the anti-racism movement must grow stronger.

Almost 700 people attended the conference which launched a charter against racism

We must build the basis for unity, not concentrate on structures and committees and other mistakes of the past,' he said.

The Brent East Labour MP warned that 'the objective conditions in which racism and fascism grow will increase.'

It was a remarkable fact that Britain was now at the top of its economic cycle – 'this is as good as it gets.'

The assembly was punctuated with moving scenes among victims of racism and those who had fought back.

The small swollen-faced figure of Asian student Mukhtar Ahmed who was beaten by a gang of racist thugs rose high on the platform to declare simply: 'We can crack it'.

Next to him sat Kelly Turner, the white teenager who defied her racist peers and gave evidence against one of the gang who attacked him.

'We should stand together. Racism is not right. If I had to do it again, I would,' she said to rousing applause.

Neville Lawrence, whose school boy son was knifed to death on the streets of south London appealed for the Kelly Turners in his own area to come out of the shadows.

Black people had lost patience with the police and the criminal justice system. 'We've got to find ways of persuading the police and the Crown Prosecution Service to take action,' he said.

Local MP Peter Shore said that racist propaganda must be banned. There had only been a handful of prosecutions under existing legislation.

But the law couldn't do everything. There needed to be a government elected that was 'was willing to take social deprivation head on.'

TUC general secretary John Monks announced that there would be a union-backed march in the north of England in the spring, building on last year's 50,000-strong TUC Unite Against Racism demonstration through the East End.

Anti-racism would be at the centre of TUC campaigning and integrated into the fight for full employment and social justice, he pledged.

Lee Jasper from the National Black Caucus urged unity between Afro-Caribbean, African and Asian peoples.

He looked forward to the day when Asian people would intervene when young Afro-Caribbean youths were stopped needlessly by the police.

He looked forward to the day when black youth from Briton would offer their support and protection on the streets of Tower Hamlets.

And he looked forward to the day when 'white English people carried anti-racism around in their back pockets like a bible.'

Mr Jasper urged people to discuss, debate and test the draft charter in action before returning to a new assembly to adopt it.

© *The Morning Star*
February, 1995

INDEX

ADDITIONAL RESOURCES

You might like to contact the following organisations for further information. Due to the increasing cost of postage, many organisations cannot respond to inquiries unless they receive a stamped, addressed envelope.

Association of Black Social Workers and Allied Professionals
Unit 228
Bon March Building
London SW9 8EJ
Tel: 0171 738 5603

CAFOD (Catholic Fund for Overseas Development)
Romero Close
Stockwell Road
London SW9 9TY
Tel: 0171 733 7900

Campaign Against Racist Laws
15 Kenton Avenue
Southall
Middlesex UB1 3QF
Tel: 0181 571 1437

Catholic Association for Racial Justice (CARJ)
St Vincents Community Centre
Talma Road
London SW2 1AS
Tel: 0171 274 0024

Children's Legal Centre
20 Crompton Terrace
London
N1 2UN
Tel: 0171 359 9392

Commission for Racial Equality (CRE)
10 - 12 Allington Street
London SW1E 5EH
Tel: 0171 828 7022

Churches Commission on Racial Justice
Interchurch House
London
SE1 7RC
Tel: 0171 620 4444

Immigration Aid Unit
400 Cheetham Hill Road
Manchester 8
Tel: 0161 740 7722

Institute of Race Relations
2-6 Leeke Street
London WC1X 9HS
Tel: 0171 837 0041

Joint Council of Welfare & Immigrants
115 Old Street
London EC1V 9JR
Tel: 0171 251 8706/8

Libertarian Alliance
25 Chapter Chambers
Esterbrook Street
London SW1P 4NN
Tel: 0171 821 5502

Minority Rights Group Ltd
Education Department
379 Brixton Road
London SW9 7DE
Tel: 0171 978 9498

National Anti-racist Movement in Education (NAME)
41 Strawberry Lane
Carshalton
Surrey SM5 2NG
Tel: 0181 670 4488

National Children's Bureau
8 Wakely Street
London EC1V 7QE
Tel: 0171 843 6000

National Youth Agency
17-23 Albion Street
Leicester LE1 6GD
Tel: 01533 471200

NCH Action for Children
85 Highbury Park
London N5 1UD
Tel: 0171 226 2033
Fax: 0171 226 2537

Newham Monitoring Project
382 Katherine Street
London E7 8NW
Tel: 0181 552 6284

Race Relations Unit
Birmingham City Council
3 Congreve Passage
Birmingham B3 3DA
Tel: 0121 235 2545

Refugee Forum
54 Tavistock Place
London WC1H 9RG

Runnymede Trust
11 Princelet Street
London E1 6QH
Tel: 0171 375 1496

Searchlight
37B New Cavendish Street
London W1 8JR
Tel: 0171 274 4040

Trade Union Congress – Equal Rights Department
Congress House
23-28 Great Russell Street
London WC1B 3LS
Tel: 0171 284 4040

Transport and General Workers Union – Equalities Officer
Transport House
Smith Square
London SW1P 3JB
Tel: 0171 828 7788

The Anti-Racist Alliance
PO Box 150
London WC1X 9AT
Tel: 0171 278 6869

Women's International League for Peace and Freedom (British Section) (WILPF)
157 Lyndhurst Road
Worthing
Sussex BN11 2DG
Tel: 01903 205161

SOUTH DEVON COLLEGE
LIBRARY

ACKNOWLEDGEMENTS

The publisher is grateful for permission to reproduce the following material.

Chapter One: Discrimination

Racism and its roots, © CAFOD – On the side of people in need, January 1995, *Race – the facts*, © New Internationalist, October 1994, *Without prejudice*, © Commission for Racial Equality/BBC Radio 1, June 1994, *We may be Black but please don't call us British*, © The Voice, 24th January 1995 page 9, *'They all look the same to me . . .'*, © SCADU, Janury 1995, *What is the Commission for Racial Equality?*, © Commission for Racial Equality, January 1995, *Restaurants to pay £30m to victims of racism*, © AFP, 26th May 1994, *Blacks stranded at back of jobs queue*, © The Observer, 12th February 1994, *Equality for all*, © Transport and General Workers Union, June 1993, *Report explodes A-level myth*, © The Voice, 13th September 1994 page 17, *It's no joke when you can't get a job*, © Commission for Racial Equality/ BBC Radio 1, June 1994, *Ministers admit 60% of young black men jobless*, © The Independent, 20th January 1995, *The Wood-Sheppard principles*, © Churches Commission for Racial Justice, January 1995, *Wanted: ombudsman for racial minorities*, © The Independent, 17th November 1994 page 20, *Harassment or law enforcement?*, © The Voice, February 1995, *Whitewash*, © The Economist, June 1994, *Black people more likely to be stopped by police*, © The Voice, January 1995, *EU warned of growing racism*, © The Guardian, 17th November 1994 page 17, *No room for racism*, © Commission for Racial Equality/BBC Radio 1, June 1994, *Anger over UN investigation into racism in Britain*, © The Times, 12th December 1994 page 6.

Chapter Two: Racial Violence

Living with violence, © Churches Commission for Racial Justice, January 1995, *Reported race attacks double in five years*, © The Independent, 18th March 1994, *Stay and stand*, © The Guardian, 12th October 1994 page 6, *Sticks and stones may break my bones, but words . . .*, © Commission for Racial Equality/BBC Radio 1, June 1994, *An everyday story of racial hatred*, © The Guardian, 6th July 1994, page 10, *Home Secretary opposes demand for new law on racist violence*, © The Asian Times, 8th October 1994 page 2, *The campaign*, © Commission for Racial Equality, 1994, *A 9-point action plan for football clubs*, © Commission for Racial Equality, 1994, *Incidents of racial attacks and violence in Britain*, © HMSO Reprinted with the kind permission of the Controller of Her Majesty's Stationery Office, January, 1995, *Scotland the intolerable*, © The Herald, 25th January 1995, *Flames of hate*, © Commission for Racial Equality/BBC Radio 1, June 1994, *Racism won't affect our goals*, © The Independent, 25th January 1995 page 22, *Britons are born . . . and born white*, © The Guardian, 5th October, *Dealing with hate*, © Community Care, 9-5 June page 11, *Racial attacks and incidents*, © Commission for Racial Equality, Annual Report 1993 page 25, *Report finds evidence of racial harassment in rural England*, © The Guardian, 8th December 1994, *Racist violence must be ended*, © CRE Connections, Commission for Racial Equality, January 1995 No 3 page 1, *Statistics on racial incidents*, © CRE Connections, Commission for Racial Equality, Summer 1994 No 1 page 10, *MEP demands ban on fascists*, © Morning Star, 6 February 1995.

Photographs and illustrations

Page 1: CAFOD, pages 3, 8, 14, 28: Ken Pyne, pages 4, 19, 20, 22, 26, 30, 34: Folio Collective, pages 7, 12, 17, 18, 21, 24, 32: David Hoffman, page 7: Commission for Racial Equality (CRE).

Craig Donnellan
Cambridge
April, 1995

SOUTH DEVON COLLEGE
LIBRARY